AMERICAN WINNERS OF THE
NOBEL LITERARY PRIZE

AMERICAN WINNERS OF THE NOBEL LITERARY PRIZE

★ ★ ★

Edited by Warren G. French and Walter E. Kidd

UNIVERSITY OF OKLAHOMA PRESS

NORMAN

LIBRARY OF CONGRESS CATALOG CARD NUMBER: 67–24622

Copyright 1968 by the University of Oklahoma Press, Publishing Division of the University. Composed and printed at Norman, Oklahoma, U.S.A., by the University of Oklahoma Press. First edition.

To the memory of

ALAN SWALLOW

(1915–1966)

editor, educator, writer
for his unique and invaluable services
to modern American writers.
He cannot be replaced.

CONTENTS

vii

AMERICAN WINNERS OF THE
NOBEL LITERARY PRIZE

INTRODUCTION
by Walter E. Kidd

O F THE FIVE international awards established by Swedish industrialist Alfred Nobel in his will drawn in 1895, the Nobel Prize in Literature has from the beginning presented difficulties to the awards committee. Nobel's will directed that it be given to "the person who shall have produced in the field of literature the most outstanding work of an idealistic tendency," and that it be administered by "the Academy in Stockholm"—the Swedish Academy.

While the monetary award is substantial, the prestige which accompanies it is enormous. And whether the honorees have always been worthy from a literary standpoint has been debatable. It is suspected that on occasion dissensions within the Academy have made compromises necessary, as in 1908 when German philosopher Rudolf Eucken was chosen over Adolf Harnack, Swinburne, and Selma Lagerlöf. Moreover, the interpretation of the term "work of idealistic tendency" has been subject to discussion and change, as has the decision concerning whether to honor an author for a single work or for the whole body of his works.

Since the first literary award in 1901, seven Americans have been honored by the Academy. This book is concerned with these American winners of the prize, an assessment of the literary value of their writing both before and after receiving it, and a consideration of other close contenders or candidates. The qualities primarily responsible for the award to each of the American writers honored from 1930 to 1962 are appraised, and attention is drawn to the qualities in American writing that have come to be regarded as most significant in contemporary culture.

The chapters discussing honorees are arranged chronologically according to the year of the award:

Sinclair Lewis (1885–1951)	1930
Eugene O'Neill (1888–1953)	1936
Pearl Buck (1892–)	1938
T. S. Eliot (1888–1965)	1948
William Faulkner (1897–1962)	1949
Ernest Hemingway (1898–1961)	1954
John Steinbeck (1902–)	1962

However, each subject's technical, psychological, spiritual, and ideological kinships with and differences from the other honorees and the runners-up, as well as his part in the literary continuity of the United States, are not necessarily discussed according to such chronology. His significance and books are analyzed and evaluated but not dissected as in a history of literature. Each chapter also explores the extent of the winner's pertinent contribution to and exemplification of the main literary trends in the twentieth century, especially between 1914 and 1960.

4

Biographical data are included only when the details are essential to validate or illuminate the appraisal. The writer's literary career up to the date of the Nobel recognition and the books and reasons probably responsible for the international salute are examined. His writing career following the honor is sketched, with comments on whether or not he has declined or progressed in his writing. Furthermore, whenever feasible, the critic examines the winner's qualifications for the tribute versus the claims of the runners-up—such as Sinclair Lewis versus Theodore Dreiser and James Branch Cabell; Pearl Buck versus Edith Wharton, Willa Cather, and Ellen Glasgow; T. S. Eliot versus Robert Frost, Ezra Pound, and Wallace Stevens; and John Steinbeck versus John Dos Passos and James T. Farrell. When reflecting on the claims of the runners-up, critics usually recall that Mark Twain, Henry James, and William Dean Howells, though all were eligible candidates, were not so honored.

The winners, with the exception of Pearl Buck—the moral mother, a late-Victorian who champions old-fashioned values in a mixed-up age of futility and despair—represent most of the literary trends in modern America and the force of literary change through the energized renewal of traditional technique and thought or through the dynamics of revolt in this era of skepticism and lustiness.

All these authors—Pearl Buck again excepted—express the pervasive disillusion and pessimism during and between the two world wars. Bitter disillusion, neurotic behavior, spiritual sterility, and physical and psychological ruthlessness of an industrialized society mark their writings. Eliot's secular wasteland poems imply the impotency of spiritual hollowness and psychopathic evils in a civilization without true religion, especially in the commercialized city com-

5

plexes. In *The Sun Also Rises* (1926) and *A Farewell to Arms* (1929), Ernest Hemingway tough-mindedly but tragically directs his cynicism at the victors of World War I for losing the peace aimed at making the world safe for democracy. In his best novels—all written in the Roaring Twenties—Sinclair Lewis, with satiric and reportorial realism, ridicules "dullness made God," Babbittry in business, tawdry reactionism in politics and society, and shabby hypocrisy and confused moral standards in religion. In *Strange Interlude*, Eugene O'Neill, with Strindbergian realism or naturalism, dramatizes the crack-up of American morality, and in *The Hairy Ape*, the ominous and profane dissociation between the worker and society. The resulting defeatism and portentousness are epitomized by Elmer Rice, a contemporary of O'Neill, in *The Adding Machine*, an expressionistic tragedy that damns the reducing of men to mechanized puppets in a dehumanized machine age.

During the Great Depression, condemning America becomes rapidly more iconoclastic and aggressive. In his writings of the period William Faulkner gothically delineates the perverting and crumbling of the South's prewar aristocratic splendor in this brutal and fragmenting era. James T. Farrell in *Studs Lonigan* relentlessly and sordidly details the breakdown of middle-class morality. Almost epically John Steinbeck chronicles the unrelieved suffering of uprooted Americans in his proletarian novel *The Grapes of Wrath*. He, as well as O'Neill, Faulkner, Hemingway, and even Pearl Buck in *The House of Earth* unconsciously, reveals that socio-economic-chemical determinism degrades the individual's thinking and drives and victimizes him into blind animalism. *U.S.A.* by John

6

Dos Passos and *Studs Lonigan* by James T. Farrell verbally photograph slices of raw life in the industrialized areas, thus documenting how inner and outer forces overwhelm man, producing a soulless, helpless mass on the animal level.

However, intellectual currents, most of them drawing from the literary heritage, lessen the severity of the prevailing pessimism. After receiving the Nobel salute, Faulkner soon becomes the "public Faulkner" and, consequently, increasingly urgent and strident, providing more of a moral language than in his early writings. Although Steinbeck writes with scientific inductiveness or naturalism and with allegorical realism at times, he finds ultimate virtue in man's obeying the biological urge to reproduce mainly for the survival of humanity. Beyond this, Steinbeck sometimes meditates mystically on the cosmic unity of the universe and on the holy unity of nature and of all that lives. In *The Grapes of Wrath*, Casy finds that he and the hills are mysteriously akin and that "all that lives is holy." Into his sense perceptions Steinbeck fuses his affectionate intuition, a sort of primitive reverence of ultimately mysterious nature to which all things belong. This compassionate reflection is rather complementary to Robert Frost's intimate love of man and earth and his golden-mean but untranscendental reflection on the universe. There are vibrant humanism and love of soil and people in the writings of Willa Cather and Ellen Glasgow and implications of constructive triumph and durable affirmation of the stronghearted.

Lewis has no facility for profound or artistic innovation, but he is alertly humane in his manifold Americanness and his imaginative moralizing. Yet not even in his later works does he become so intent upon sermonizing, as Steinbeck does after 1945, that he enfeebles his humanism or his narrative zest and his impish, often impious satire on human conditions.

In his speech accepting the Nobel award Lewis prophetically states that Hemingway is a worthy Nobel candidate and emphasizes that the duty of the American writer is to express life truthfully, not to prettify it. Distinctively, Hemingway tells the truth, first about the American experience, then about the European experience, and finally about the human experience, with intense precision and firm verbal economy.

Another positive force in this disjointed age of technological impacts and changes is the religious faith illuminated in Willa Cather's *Death Comes for the Archbishop* and in Eliot's Christian poems and verse plays, which adeptly deal with the intelligent search for personal identity and intimate contact with *being* itself. Each of his plays is a spiritual and difficult striving to attain holiness. In *House of Earth, Fighting Angel,* and *The Exile,* Pearl Buck has a Whitmanesque belief in the individual's importance and Christian confidence in the aspiration of man toward a universal unity of brotherhood, a steady faith in democratic humanity in progressive civilization, including a humanitarian balance between body and soul. Like Willa Cather and Edith Wharton, she perceives universal goodness innate in the particulars of existence. However, after her Nobel award, Mrs. Buck's preoccupation with humanitarianism becomes so obsessive, at times even sentimental and easily optimistic, that she negates her artistic objectivity with popularized didacticism and propaganda for humanitarian reforms.

In keeping with her easy affirmation of the innate goodness of man, so contrary to the attitude of this age of anxiety, is Mrs. Buck's rejection of modern techniques such as the stream-of-consciousness, symbolism, and deep psychological probing into man's behavior. Up to the mid-century there is evident variety, not only in subject matter and attitudes, but also in writing techniques and experimentation in poetry, fiction, and drama.

The American poetry of the modern era is the most vibrantly varied genre. It involves much meaningful rebellion, experimentation, and innovation in the use of diction, structural techniques, rhythms, tones, and the psychology of Freud and Jung. In keeping with the writers' revolt against Victorian smugness, strait-laced conventions, platitudinous optimism, and imperialism, the American poets, especially from 1912 to the 1930's, reject the rigid sobriety toward the functions of poetry, toward traditional verse patterns, conventional poetic language, and clichés incompatible with this century, toward puritanical taboos against certain aspects of human drives, and toward subject matter judged uncouth and indecent.

Ironically and probingly aware of the individual victimized by the indifferent and brutal universe and of the ironic, at times tragic, incongruities, and the incompatible values in the complex confusion and violence of this era, the poets use the logic of their imagination to try to give connotative order to the denotative disorder of particulars to suggest a universal unity and logic, both physical and divine, in the world today.

The poet seeks variation in verse patterns and concrete words from ordinary speech to energize conventional language with living expressions true to the poet and his age and to fuse thought and emotion. But whenever it is neces-

9

sary to express the complicated age more effectively, the poet may advisedly dislocate the language or put aside the vernacular simplicity. Also, the poet seeks organic rhythm or cadence, ranging from the free verse of Edgar Lee Masters, John Gould Fletcher, and E. E. Cummings to the comparatively traditional technique of Edwin Arlington Robinson, who, indirectly influenced by the new poetic freedom, varies from the artificially regular verse forms, diction, and rhythms of the nineteenth century. Robert Frost, more than Robinson, deviates from the strict metrical forms and, in a number of his poems, from the conventional stanzaic patterns. His wisely controlled innovations naturally but poetically fuse traditional meters and free-verse cadences in keeping with colloquial rhythms and tones. Expertly and much more eruditely and symbolically than Frost, T. S. Eliot, who innovates by making his poetic language easy and colloquial in an intelligent and dramatic way, uses a subtly and precisely regulated semi-free verse and becomes the most technically influential literary figure among American poets of this century. He accurately selects the concrete words from the American vernacular to express his poetic conceptions with unadorned erudition, sensitive and ironic impact, and intense originality. His symbolic obtuseness and his academic literary allusions are not deliberate obscurities, but are obtuse because the wasteland era is intricate and often obscure. His idiomatic tone and logic and his insight into primitive depths are usually direct and cynically informal. Eliot, as well as such prominent poets as Ezra Pound, Edwin Arlington Robinson, Wallace Stevens, William Carlos Williams, and Hart Crane, varies from the vernacular simplicities to express complicated meanings. Eliot and Pound are the most dominant influences, in many ways unfortunately academic.

Among American poets of fine potentials enticed into the regimentation of universities and colleges between 1935 and 1960 and partially sterilized are Randall Jarrell, Delmore Schwartz, Peter Viereck, Robert Lowell, Theodore Roethke, Conrad Pendleton, and Richard Wilbur. Each, to a varying degree, bleakly stresses discontinuity, violence, and frustrations. Assuredly the achievement of none of them parallels the greatness of Eliot, Pound, Robinson, Stevens, and Hart Crane. Their poetry lacks the power, creative passion, and high seriousness of great poetry.

The rising generation of poets, subsidized protégés of higher institutions, are committed to textbook regulations and assembly-line workshops for writers. Such pedantry fosters in these poets an ivory-tower intellectualism and isolation and obsessive preoccupation with tortured and often fake originality, rhetorical dishonesty, fractured rhythms, knotted imagery, contrived ambiguities, farfetched references, and dissociated oddities. This pedantry also indoctrinates them against the dynamics of life and its living heritage, and thereby isolates them from the paradoxical age of industrial utility and scientific marvels, of paranoiac violence and global jitters, of nightmare guilt and negative disillusion. They have lost vital contact with the contemporary world, and lack, as a result, undespairing stamina to probe the universal dynamics in the present dehumanized pessimism and to acquire the creative courage to transcend the anxieties and torments, the terror and the glory of Creation, and to understand the crucial struggle between human will and deterministic forces. Only by facing this era wisely can they assume the sacred trust of reinterpreting the practical, ethical, and spiritual truths that, reanimated once again, will help to guide, quicken, and motivate the splendid discoveries of science and fuse them into the collective enterprise, humanism, and aestheticism of America and help to integrate the basic achievements of this era into the nation's heritage.

Modern American drama, reflecting the lively technical variety of playwriting and staging and the fermenting thoughts typical of the modern era, especially the revolt against conventional taboos, flourishes in the Roaring Twenties. During this dynamic decade Eugene O'Neill emerges as the dominant playwright among a group of famous ones. His domination continues to 1950. His best plays are memorable achievements.

Viewing life tragically and exploring man's failures and his need for God or at least for humanistic guidance, O'Neill gives dramatic expression and universality to American particulars by deepening his insight into the psyche and human psychology and by using his poetic imagination and organic romanticism in unroutine patterns. By triumphantly intensifying his dramatic artistry, he becomes a vital influence on his contemporaries.

Like Lewis, Faulkner, Hemingway, and Steinbeck, O'Neill and his fellow dramatists—Maxwell Anderson, Robert Sherwood, DuBose Heyward, Elmer Rice, Clifford Odets, Arthur Miller, Tennessee Williams, and Edward Albee—are intensely concerned with psychological, ethical, and ideological problems, especially man's tragic maladjustment and the ironic loneliness and defeat of the individual futilely striving to adjust to a society in which he is considered unimportant. Also, they are concerned with the

12

new stage techniques, with the use of authentic American speech imagery, tones, and cadence. They employ expressionistic technique, stream-of-consciousness, and other revolutionary innovations—naturalism, primitivism, and the views of Freud, Jung, Nietzsche, and Marx. Such plays as *The Hairy Ape, Desire Under the Elms, The Emperor Jones,* and *Mourning Becomes Electra,* by O'Neill, *What Price Glory,* by Maxwell Anderson and Laurence Stallings, *The Adding Machine,* by Elmer Rice, *The Glass Menagerie,* by Tennessee Williams, and *Death of a Salesman,* by Arthur Miller, are representative of the predominant techniques, disillusion, ideological and Freudian ferments, violence, human frustrations, and chronic confusion of this disorderly era. O'Neill's last plays, *The Iceman Cometh* and *Long Day's Journey into Night,* along with the best plays of his previous years make the Nobel award justified and inevitable and mark him as a major contributor to American and world literature.

The novels of Lewis, Buck, Faulkner, Hemingway, and Steinbeck have little plot structure, but, instead, many details, sometimes photographic and documentary, to depict contemporary life truthfully and realistically. Like Lewis, the others usually employ biographical or autobiographical chronicling. So do Theodore Dreiser, F. Scott Fitzgerald, James T. Farrell, Thomas Wolfe, John Dos Passos, Erskine Caldwell, and Vardis Fisher.

All these fictionists realistically present the particulars of American scenes, characters, and life, except Hemingway, whose novels picture foreign backgrounds, and Mrs. Buck, whose best work, *House of Earth,* treats the Chinese peasants and their native environment, objectively narrating a social and political revolution and implying the universal life forces and values and the eternal verities of earth and its seasons.

These five writers seldom comment on characters as the nineteenth-century novelist did. They consistently remain objective, presenting the characters through dialogue, behavior, and thoughts. Like Hemingway, Steinbeck is often primitivistic in his psychology, especially in portraying characters close to the animal level. These authors reveal that disintegration, vulgarity, and other evils of society are the results of the disorderly process of life. Although naturalistic in his writings, Steinbeck maintains his popularity even in the present but fails to produce work equal to his best novels, *Of Mice and Men, The Grapes of Wrath*, and *Cannery Row*. Because he projects his metaphysical vision and his collective sympathy for the exploited "little man," his humanism at times emerges vibrantly out of the mechanistic determinism of the industrialized world and its social and economic cataclysm.

Recent impressive novels evidence, not a tawdry end, but a decline to a period of difficult transition, synthesizing dissociated elements and confusions brought about by the maladjusting impact of technology and puritanic prudery upon man, and partly assimilating the literary influences of Faulkner, Hemingway, O'Neill, Steinbeck, and Eliot to search for a new organic way of enriching the language and giving order to chaotic experience. To approach the stature of these Nobel Prize winners, the young writers must learn to comprehend their inner and outer experiences in this age. To interpret authentically the unmeasurable and measurable facets of experience, they need to clarify their own visions, to relate their art to the fundamental actions that eventually help to organize political, economic, social, moral, or ethical matters, and to moderate excessive subjectivism and pornography.

A few recent fiction writers of much literary talent seeking to identify themselves and their writing with this fractured age are Norman Mailer, John Barth, William Styron, James Baldwin, Jack Kerouac, John Updike, William Burroughs, Joseph Heller, Truman Capote, and J. D. Salinger; but whether any of them will attain greatness comparable to that of Faulkner and Hemingway remains to be seen.

SINCLAIR LEWIS

by Robert J. Griffin

*"There it was, complete, literature: the
crude fact immortalized."*

THE IMMEDIATE, practical, and public reasons for Lewis'
receiving the prize are not hard to find. At the Nobel Festi-
val on December 10, 1930, the permanent secretary of the
Swedish Academy, Erik Axel Karlfeldt, gave a brief ex-
planatory address; clearly his descriptions of the major
novels and the achievement of this "pioneer" American
novelist expressed the official understanding and evaluation
of the Academy. Nearly three decades later in his book-
length study of *The Swedish Acceptance of American
Literature*, Carl L. Anderson was able to show in per-
suasive detail the cultural factors involved in the choice of
the first American laureate.

Karlfeldt's commentary was necessarily sketchy, and his
emphases were hardly unpredictable. He began quite
naturally with the sociological approach. In praising *Main
Street* as a superior "description of life in a small town," he
observed that the novelist's complex attitude embraced
both nostalgic tolerance and a sense of outrage at "ugliness
and bigotry." Zenith, the site of most of the action of

16

Babbitt, was described as "a hundred times richer in 100 per cent Americanism and a hundred times as large as Gopher Prairie and, therefore, a hundred times as satisfied with itself, and the enchantment of its optimism and progressive spirit is embodied in George F. Babbitt." There is clear irony in Karlfeldt's terms for the qualities that *Babbitt* represents, but the Swedish poet may have startled some of his audience—or may have caused some to wonder if the Academy knew what it was doing—when he said, "It is probable that Babbitt approaches the ideal of an American popular hero of the middle class." Although the remainder of Karlfeldt's remarks on *Babbitt* suggests that all his favorable terms were intended to work in an at least partly unfavorable way, he may have meant here again to indicate Lewis' complexity of attitude. At any rate, he was unarguably right when he proceeded to note the novel's central concern with the reductivism of modern standardization, the commercial mystique of salesmanship and its inevitable corollary, "an earthbound but at the same time pompous utilitarianism." He also noted what he called Lewis' "unparalleled gift of words."

When he turned to *Arrowsmith,* Karlfeldt called it a "work of a more serious nature," presumably because it has a more admirable hero, because medicine and the sciences in general are more serious affairs than selling—even when selling has become a kind of religion—and because the "book is full of admirable learning which is certified by experts as accurate." Praise was bestowed on the realism of Martin Arrowsmith's character, as well as on the variety of personalities portrayed and the extensive delineation of modern medical science in all its aspects. (Karlfeldt suggested that Lewis himself was a semi-scientist in his always careful "study of details.") But if the Academy was impressed with the verisimilitude of the idealistic Arrowsmith's mistakes or imperfections, the characterization of the antihero in *Elmer Gantry* would have to be acclaimed on different grounds. Although Karlfeldt began by likening this "big novel" to a "surgical operation on one of the most delicate parts of the social body," he soon made it clear that the novel's excellence lay not in the realms of delicacy or finesse but in satiric force: "the book is a feat of strength, genuine and powerful, and its full-flavored, sombre satire has a devastating effect."

Dodsworth was the last novel published before the awarding of the prize. In its title character Karlfeldt discerned yet another version of the American "hero," a kind of aristocratic businessman capable of serious reflection and not unaware of his European roots. A true "American, but not a jingo," Dodsworth is attracted to both the stability of the Old World and the robust pragmatism of the New; "when he returns [to America], we understand that the heart of Sinclair Lewis follows him." For in his distinctive fiction Lewis "is an American," and the action of the Academy signalized international recognition of the fact that the "new great American literature has started with national self-criticism."

There were those at the time who felt that the Academicians smacked their lips a bit too loudly over the critical pungency of Lewis' work. Carl Anderson's book has shown that these feelings were well founded. Prior to World War I, the Swedish assessment of American literature, reasonably typical of a general European attitude, was not very favorable. After the Allied victory and Wilson's emergence as a respected international leader, estimation of the arts in

America began to improve, and in the twenties the translations of Sinclair Lewis' works enjoyed a remarkable success. Yet this success did not represent a change in the Swedish opinion of American cultural attainment. As the qualifications of Karlfeldt's praise indicate, Europe was ready to acknowledge the achievement of American writers because the writers acknowledged deficiencies in the achievement of America. It is perhaps ironic and sad that our literature had to gain serious international esteem through the back door of sociological criticism, which was really through a confirming of old prejudices. Eventually this means of entry would hardly matter. Once the "acceptance" became a fact, the diversity of American letters would be considered more fully, the grounds of the acceptance more realistically broadened. Meanwhile, however, there was the initial circumstance of the acceptance to be enacted: there was Sinclair Lewis in Stockholm, radiantly grateful, surprisingly modest and self-effacing, but quite ready to speak his mind. Much of his Nobel address was devoted to celebrating the emergence in America of a "literature worthy of her vastness," but he characteristically saw fit to set his praise in a framework directed at what he considered to be narrow, reactionary, and unhealthily genteel in the respectable literary circles of the United States, and it was this latter aspect of his address which received the most attention in the European press. Here at last was that robust doubter—the man determined to undermine smugness and give unreflecting patriotism its proper setback— which the Old World critics had vigorously called for but only faintly expected.

I do not mean to imply that Sinclair Lewis was lionized

purely and simply for his scoffing. Although discussion of his work did as a rule stress its satiric or social-critical import, it should go without saying that the literary committee of the Academy took its responsibility too seriously to select a writer merely because he was willing to find faults where they were convinced faults lay. The official citation specified that the 1930 Nobel Prize in literature was given to "Sinclair Lewis for his powerful and vivid art of description and his ability to use wit and humour in the creation of original characters." Lewis was the first writer to be elected the first time he was nominated—and when the choice was announced there was in Europe as little protest as there has ever been. The American outcries about a "national insult" were judged, by British as well as Continental intellectuals, hardly worth notice; if forceful muckraking had been the only criterion, the prize would most likely have gone to Upton Sinclair. It went instead to a novelist who was widely appreciated as a man of significant literary achievement.

The problem is, he is not now so widely appreciated. It is not so much that Lewis' work is simply deprecated, though that may happen often enough when his name crops up nowadays in critical discussion; what gives us pause—what must make us puzzle over the permanent status of Lewis as our first Nobel laureate—is the fact that his name does not crop up very often. His novels, particularly the four or five best, still sell fairly well; they have become staples of the paperback book trade. At the same time, his stock is low among American critics, lower probably than it ever was during his lifetime, certainly much lower than it was in the early thirties when he was generally regarded as our "leading novelist." The exact how and why of this change are beyond the scope of the present discussion, but I think a preliminary survey of the novels Lewis published before he got the prize, with particular attention to their recognizably American elements, can provide significant clues about the general nature of his work and the propriety of the Swedish Academy's choice, and it may even afford some incidental hints with respect to his fall from critical favor.

Whatever else Sinclair Lewis was, he was not a brilliant flash in the pan. To be sure, he enjoyed international esteem while relatively young—he was only forty-five in 1930—and his reputation began to wane within a few years after the triumphant journey to Stockholm. There was, moreover, a perfectly obvious reason for the steady waning of his reputation: after Stockholm, Lewis never again wrote a novel as good as, say, *Arrowsmith* or *Babbitt*. Many felt that each subsequent novel was a little worse than the one before, and the last one, the posthumously published *World So Wide*, was hardly more than a regrettable rewriting of *Dodsworth* with curious parallels to *Our Mr. Wrenn*. During the last dozen or more years of his life Lewis was increasingly forced to play the pathetic role of a deposed, dishonored monarch.

But if his decline appears now to have been meteoric, his rise must still be judged slow. Some writers exhibit an early maturity of intellect and craftsmanship, or at least their early efforts bear clear signs of their later accomplishment. Young Lewis certainly wanted to be a writer, as thousands of lonely small-town girls want to be great actresses. At Yale he went through all the motions, but his creative contributions to the campus magazines are not perceptibly promising. They are for the most part undistinguished undergraduate writing, either flaccid or strained, "romantic" in the sense of sophomorically dreamy. He seems always to have had a storyteller's imagination (before he hit his stride as a professional writer, he used to sell plots to Jack London), and his early publications reveal some of the concerns, the issues and the ways of approaching them, that we find characteristic of the later works. The glimmer of great expectations, however, is fitful at best; most likely it is seen only by virtue of the optical illusion we call hindsight. Lewis was slow to develop. Indeed, "develop" is inept, for Lewis was a writer less born than self-made. Although he never quite became the kind of impeccable literary craftsman that would satisfy a James Joyce, he was incontestably a dedicated artisan, a writer who worked at his trade with uncommon determination and perseverance, with ingenuous pride and ambition, and for a while, with notable success.

His first novel, *Our Mr. Wrenn* (published in 1914), is not atypically a kind of adventure story, a "romance," carefully tethered to down-to-earth realism. Mr. Wrenn starts out as a Milquetoast. He does not end up as an absolute anti-Milquetoast. He does, within the confines of a somewhat implausible plot, undergo some plausible changes of character. The timid, solitary shoe-store clerk comes into a small inheritance that allows him to realize some of his dreams of glory, essentially dreams of traveling to exotic places. Although he does not make it to Bali, he does prudently work his way over to England on a cattle boat. In England he finds his life still drab and stultifying, until he chances to meet the pretty, chic, clever, arty Istra Nash. The torch he carries for this exotic lady is doomed to flicker out, but the torchbearing does him no harm really; it is a part of his necessary education. When he comes back to New York, although he encounters at first some of the old problems and frustrations, he gradually finds friends, a moderately promising career, and a more compatible sweetheart, a nice wholesome girl who will doubtless take good care of their vine-covered cottage. No longer *our* Mr. Wrenn, he has become his own man: the pathetic Walter Mitty has grown into a rather enviable average man. One of the native traditions in which Lewis' first hero participates is that of the Innocent Abroad, and Wrenn's story allows Lewis to present some detailed images of modern American life, especially of metropolitan life as it pertains to clerks and boardinghouse society. While Wrenn represents nothing so broad as The Typical American, he is depicted as a distinct American type.

Later in his career, when Lewis had himself become a national institution, readers were likely to assume that his facility for reproducing distinctive colloquial speech was a talent he had always had. He evidently was always something of a mimic; the written "mimicry" of vital, slangy dialogue for which he became famous, however, was not a natural gift but a gradually devised expertise. The attempts to simulate vernacular conversation in *Our Mr. Wrenn* are abortive, not much better than Negro dialogue in an old southern minstrel show. In *The Trail of the Hawk* (1915), his second novel, Lewis can be seen to have made progress toward perfecting that renowned "ear." Some of the dialogue rings true, and the chapters that are supposed to be transcripts of hero Carl Ericson's diary are almost unexceptionable. In these the idiomatic diction and phrasing, all those elements of "choice" of language which usually are not conscious choices at all, constitute an effective supplementary means of characterization.

The Trail of the Hawk is a better-written novel than Our Mr. Wrenn. It is also bigger, at once more realistic and more romantic, and more emphatically American. Lewis fashioned in Carl Ericson a hero whose career could accommodate, as Wrenn's could not, much of the diversity that characterized the United States of 1915: son of the Middle West (a "Norwegian-American"), Carl is successively a Huck Finn growing up, a naïve but curious and educable college student, a clean-cut hobo in search of adventure and self-knowledge, a vanguard aviator, an inventor-businessman, and—after a stint as a more credible courter of Istra Nash—a very loving husband. Obviously, Lewis was determined to cover a great deal of ground, and the surprising thing is that he covers much of it rather ably. Carl's peregrinations naturally range over most of the continent, including Canada and Mexico as well as Chicago, Virginia, New York City, San Francisco, and so forth. There is, furthermore, appreciable evidence that Lewis meant the course of his hero's life—from youth as a hyphenated American through pioneer adventuring to industrial flair, without loss of the questing spirit and capacity for frolic—to epitomize the progress of national history, part retrospect and part hopeful prophecy; Carl's marriage is underscored as the propitious blending of a sturdy Minnesotan and an old-family New Yorker.

The stress on the Americanness of Carl's story starts at the beginning. The American Scandinavians of the Middle West are depicted as "the New Yankees," the current version of the national pioneering ethos.

Carl was a second-generation Norwegian; American-born, American in speech, American in appearance, save for his flaxen hair and china-blue eyes; and, thanks to a flag-decked public school, overwhelmingly American in tradition. When he was born the "typical American" of earlier stocks had moved to city palaces or were marooned on run-down farms. It was Carl Ericson, not a Trowbridge or a Stuyvesant or a Lee or a Grant, who was the "typical American" of his period. It was for him to carry on the American destiny of extending the Western horizon; his to restore the wintry Pilgrim virtues and the exuberant, October, partridge-drumming days of Daniel Boone; then to add, in his own or another generation, new American aspirations for beauty.

Although the overtness of this thematic Americanness decreases later in the novel, for by then the author could assume that the reader knew how to keep score, the stress is heavy in the early chapters. Eight-year-old Carl is called the "heir-apparent to the age." When he is sixteen he is told by Bone Stillman (the "village eccentric," a humane atheist, self-taught intellectual, earthy socialist—and convenient Thoreauvian *raisonneur*) that he is "a pretty average young American." But this is no diminution; a few years later, as he is about to break free of the shackles of a typical small college "education," Carl "saw the vision of the America through which he might follow the trail like the pioneers whose spiritual descendant he was." Even the hero's happy-ending marriage to a beautiful heiress has distinct sociological overtones. The union of Carl and Ruth is projected as ultimately successful because, while they represent two spheres of existence, the new and the old (Ruth is the offspring of one of the "earlier stocks" of Americans who "had moved to city palaces"), they are not total antitheses. Ruth likes excitement and discovery, Carl has respect for established traditions, and both are opposed to mere stuffiness and whatever is superficial or meretricious. So their marriage represents a blending of the best of two American strains.

Lewis' third novel, *The Job* (1917), turns from the story of a modern American boy growing up, pioneering, and making good in a realistically moderate way, to a similar saga of a small-town girl threading her way through the difficulties of city life and a business career at the beginning of the century. With more than a few reminiscences of another heroine who had got ahead, Dreiser's Sister Carrie, Una Golden manages to make her way in what was supposed to be strictly a "man's world" and, unlike Carrie, finally manages also to make a happy marriage.

"The romance, the faith, the mystery of business"— Lewis means the phrases ironically. In delineating the ins and outs of contemporary commerce, some aspects of which he had already dealt with in *Our Mr. Wrenn* and *The Trail of the Hawk*, he is careful to puncture its self-inflated image. Yet for all his sneering at the myths of this modern frontier, he cannot help taking it seriously. He strips it of false glory, presenting some quite respectable wry analyses of the mores, caste system, and politics of the business world, but he is as much attracted to as repelled by what amounts to a proud and powerful way of life. Una Golden, as an "Average Young Woman on a Job" (Lewis' capitals) and later as an unaverage successful *entrepreneuse*, is one of many "creating a new age." Seen especially as a new American age, the world of *The Job* was bound to appeal to Lewis' taste for national adventure, and the novel turns out to be much more romance than exposé. This is not to say that the book is a failure, for it was not intended to be sweeping satire. Although the fictional structure may buckle and sag—none of the first five novels are better than very good second-rate fiction—the historical portions are sturdy. Lewis was clearly maturing as a social chronicler. When he introduces cultural analysis into *The Job*, he does so with subtler art and a kind of modest authoritativeness far preferable to the awkward intrusions of rather banal sociology that marred some of the earlier work. He was, moreover, developing an acerbic wit capable of flashing out now and again with telling effect. And he was becoming a better writer. *The Job* contains fewer passages that are callowly cute or grandiose; it reveals more of a gift for the genuine, penetrating, ungarnished *aperçu*.

Lewis was coming of age as a novelist, but not altogether willingly. In the dedicatory introduction to his next book, *The Innocents* (1917), he expressed his "strident admiration" for a number of contemporary British realists, including Compton Mackenzie, Hugh Walpole, D. H. Lawrence, and most notably "their master and teacher" H. G. Wells; but he also made it clear that he found the mantle of authorial maturity uncomfortable. "Ponderous realism" was the way he characterized his serious work to date, as though he had become more adept at social realism than he cared to admit. He had previously published a pseudonymous novel for boys, *Hike and the Aeroplane* (1912), but that had been simply a potboiler written for the publisher who employed him as a manuscript reader. *The Innocents* was something else, an admitted attempt to lay aside the serious writing he was mastering for "a flagrant excursion, a tale for people who still read Dickens and clip out spring poetry and love old people and children." Heaven knows it was flagrant—

an outrageously sentimental tale of an old couple who sink to trampdom only to rise to the glories of small-town respectability. The social realist peeps through from time to time to remark the "three sorts of native New Yorkers" or the vagaries of "chaotically competitive business." There is, however, much more sweetness than light, and in its own innocent way the book has a certain charm. It would be ungenerous to begrudge Lewis this ingenuous exercise in self-indulgence.

In *Free Air* (1919), Lewis presumably means to return to his efforts at a comprehensive American realism, writing for instance of traveling salesmen as "pioneers in spats." Yet the novel is strangely more like *The Innocents*, or at least more like *Our Mr. Wrenn*, than *The Job*, as if once having let the sentimental side of his nature take precedence he could not quite get back into the groove of skeptical social commentary. Claire Boltwood and her father are motoring across the country from their town house in Brooklyn Heights to visit relatives in Seattle (shades of the pioneers' westering). Along the way they meet Milt Daggett, a self-employed mechanic in a small town in Minnesota. All manner of mishaps and adventures ensue as they cross the rest of the country. The social classes clash, and only after the direct vicissitudes in Seattle do the two young people resolve to face together "the anxieties and glories of a changing world." Of course Milt is not an ordinary mechanic; he is inventive, sensibly ambitious, a "young poet . . . rhymeless and inarticulate" but thoroughly capable of learning. "He's the real American. He has imagination and adaptability."

Milt Daggett, in fact, is another of Lewis' contributions to a long line of national heroes, one of the species that R. W. B. Lewis has so capably described in *The American*

Adam: an independent man, for all practical purposes without a past, in the process of making a better life on whatever "frontiers" of adventure may be available in his age. Carl Ericson of *The Trail of the Hawk* was a more distinctive version of the Adamic type, since he was more clearly a heroic figure of great innocence and great potentialities (at one point he actually has to contend with a temptress named Eve, but of course he is proof against her wiles), self-reliant and self-propelling in his will to move forward in the vanguard of a new history. Yet Daggett, too, is within the species, in his freedom from encumbering tradition and his willingness to venture as he representatively molds a better experience. He could have been a more convincing specimen; his paths to advancement, such as the study of engineering in an ordinary academic framework, are scarcely the sort to tax credulity. The "romance" of his achievement with Claire by his side is set in the future, with plenty of realistic dull spots allowed for in their adventuring through life. But it does not work. While the patches of cultural illustration are reasonably strong, the old thin spots in Lewis' fictional fabric have worn through.

For one thing, the happy union of disparate levels of American society is more obviously unequal to its intended symbolic function. In *The Trail of the Hawk*, Lewis was sufficiently adroit in handling the problems of the "mixed marriage" to suggest that the couple would manage to work things out and, indeed, that the success of their marriage could serve as an emblem for the viable harmony of seemingly discordant elements in the diversity of American culture. In *Free Air*, where the conjoining of unlikes is handled in a more cursory and even coy manner, it is too clear that the intermarriage cannot effectively represent a significant breaking down of distinctions. Milt and Claire are so atypical of their classes that their living more or less happily ever after can signify little if anything beyond their own good luck. Of course a part of Lewis' message may be that it is the individual that counts, and hence traditional arbitrary distinctions are meaningless, but the effect of the couple's story is that only these two individuals are truly individual; they appear to be unique rather than representative, and the strata they come from remain distinct. An inadvertent peek into the fabled melting pot reveals something disturbingly similar to pousse-café.

There is another, more embarrassing aspect to Lewis' treatment of the love story. Many critics have noted as a peculiar trait of our literature the characteristic resistance to the process of growing up. In *The American Adam*, R. W. B. Lewis comments on these "repeated efforts to revert to a lost childhood," and Leslie Fiedler is only one of many who have blanched at the frequency with which these efforts apply to the fictional portrayal of love. Romantic couples in Sinclair Lewis' early novels are never called "lovers" or even "sweethearts," always "playmates." Their finest, "togetherest" moments are apt to be spent hiking or wading, gamboling in the snow or in a meadow, cooking camp fare by a mountain stream, or in their most exalted mood, raptly observing a sunset. One may be happy at the end of *Free Air* that Milt and Claire can "start their drama with the distinction of being able to laugh together . . . [and] with the cosmic importance to the tedious world of believing in the romance that makes youth unquenchable," but when Claire vows that she will hazard all to marry Milt so as not to "lose the one real playmate I've ever had," one is forced to question the author's conception of what makes an ideal marriage. For Lewis, great love seems little more than a perpetuated child's game. One is forced, moreover, to consider this adolescent vision of romantic love as a corollary of Lewis' refusal to accept the full responsibility of authorial maturity.

In all of his first five novels he had been torn between his intellectual desire for social realism and his emotional proclivity for "romance," meaning adventure out of the ordinary, implying glamour, and often entailing (though certainly Lewis did not deliberately choose that it should entail) schoolboy sentimentalism. It was not impossible for these two tendencies to be reconciled, as Lewis was obviously trying to reconcile them in his attempts to show on the one hand the romance of the real state of American affairs and, on the other, the inadequacies or disadvantages which underlay the attractive surface. But he had not yet fully succeeded in reconciling them, because the romantic side of his nature kept subduing the skeptical side, kept urging him on to flagrant excursions, leading him to judge all realism inevitably ponderous. It was as if his head never quite knew what his heart was up to. The two might work in tandem, but they could not work against each other; that is, they could not if Lewis was ever to be a novelist of significant eminence. He had already become a popular success. All of his books had been favored by at least as many good reviews as bad, and they sold increasingly well. Doubtless he could keep on in the same vein and continue to make a nice living. There were highly literate readers, however, who had begun to take him seriously, seeing in the strengths of his work signs of better things to come; these readers would not be content if he failed to progress beyond the promise he had shown. Nor would Lewis himself. He could not contentedly rest on the laurels he had got for a good ear, the keen eye of a historian, and the ability to project himself into the lives of his protagonists with uncommon understanding.

The question was, could he take the final giant step: could he face up to the duplexity of his interests and make that previous weakness his greatest strength? The answer was *Main Street* (1920), which came upon the American reading public like a tornado out of the Middle West. Indeed, the initial impact of *Main Street* was so forceful that most commentators failed to note the novel's complexity. While Lewis had been acting as a member of the "Party of Hope" in the American cultural dialogue—finding cause for hope in the national facility for inventiveness and practical know-how, industrial technology and expertise, where nineteenth-century optimists had trusted in science as the liberator of the new Adam—he had also been preparing himself to expose the other side of the coin, national smugness, a willingness to take material achievement as an end in itself without care for the arts and the human spirit. For several years he had been tinkering with the idea for a book, called initially "The Village Virus," revealing the varieties of pettiness and foolish complacency that hid behind the myth of the small-town paradise. It was this book—this satiric exposé and nothing more—that many commentators seemed to take *Main Street* for.

At the time, *Main Street* may have appeared to represent an about-face in Lewis' professional attitude. From the celebration of national potentialities he had turned to the castigation of national failings, from social commentary to social criticism. This was not a total about-face: it was a shift in emphasis. The early works were essentially novels of illumination, fictions intended to illustrate the reality, and the romance, of some area of modern American experience previously unexplored or insufficiently understood. In all these stories Lewis had been careful to show deficiencies as well as virtues in the national character. With *Main Street,* and thereafter, the emphasis fell more heavily on the deficiencies, for Lewis had decided that these needed more attention than the progress and expectations that virtually everyone now seemed contented with. But the criticism in his best fiction is not simple denigration or iconoclasm: it represents the optimist's disappointment at finding his hopes forestalled, and it still reflects, even in the satiric venom of *Elmer Gantry,* the humanity of outlook that had generated the initial optimism.

Although this is essentially the case with Carol Kennicott's disenchantment in her attempts to improve the world of Gopher Prairie, those who identified Carol with her creator oversimplified the texture of the novel. There is a good deal of Lewis' own values in Carol's make-up, and most of the other characters suffer by comparison with her good intentions; but to note the many imperfections of Gopher Prairie is not to prove the perfection of the heroine. Carol is often foolish. The means she chooses to serve her admirable ends are usually rash or naïve, and she herself comes finally, although somewhat imperfectly, to recognize her own shortcomings when she returns to Will a wiser wife, with more realistic hopes for making the best of a world that leaves much to be desired. Will Kennicott, by no means an unsympathetic character, represents another side of Lewis' nature; his more earthy values may not be so poignantly accented as Carol's thwarted dreams of a cultured community, but they are not to be sneered at. The truth is that, in *Main Street*, Lewis recognized his emotional-intellectual ambivalences and molded the recognition into a first-rate novel. Or, to put the matter in slightly different terms, Carol does represent the author's self, but it is a self observed and honestly depicted. Once the original hubbub over the novel had died down, critics began to remark that it was a superior work precisely because of the novelist's refusal to blink at the complexities of the book's fundamental human issues. If the acid-etched portraits of various types of small-town smugness were the more notable features of the novel's impact as a social phenomenon, the gentler ironies applied to the heroine were no less important as evidence that Lewis had at last made the grade as a mature novelist.

Within the decade inaugurated by the thoroughgoing success of *Main Street* and capped by Lewis' acceptance of the prize, he published also *Babbitt* (1922), *Arrowsmith* (1925), *Elmer Gantry* (1927), and *Dodsworth* (1929). The fact that the period included the lesser *Mantrap* (1926) and *The Man Who Knew Coolidge* (1928) can hardly prevent our judging it a brilliant decade. If it is true that Lewis never again produced a work to equal the best of this period, for our present purposes the important consideration is that he had become a novelist of undeniable insight and power. He was a personality as well as a novelist of note, as in his righteous declining of the Pulitzer Prize on the grounds that the award was too likely to encourage writers "to become safe, polite, obedient, and sterile." His reputation spread fast abroad as the novels were translated into various languages. He could not be ignored. His name was bound to come up sooner or later before the selection committee for the Nobel Prize in literature. He had, in a word, earned the prize.

I regret that I cannot give each of Lewis' five best novels the careful discussion it deserves. I have spent perhaps too much space on the earlier works, but this imbalance has seemed to me justified, for several reasons. The five best are naturally the best known and the most often written about, and these are the novels that anyone interested in Lewis will want to read and judge for himself—indeed they are well worth rereading. The remarks of Karlfeldt, the Academy secretary, reported at the beginning of this essay constitute not only the official assessment but also a valid enough thumbnail description of Lewis' finest accomplishments. I have therefore thought it my proper function to try to exhibit some of the characteristic qualities of his fiction as these emerged in the preparatory novels, those experimental efforts of his apprentice years, as well as in the more masterly products of his peak period. But this procedure should not be taken to mean that the best novels are simply improved rewrites of their predecessors. I have already mentioned an important shift of emphasis initiated by *Main Street*, from a modified optimism to a kind of enlightened muckraking. Each of the best novels is, moreover, very distinct from the rest. Lewis had not merely mastered a single theme or subject; he had become truly versatile. In the remaining paragraphs I shall, with some scant attention to the other major works, try to suggest a few more of the significant traits of Lewis' fiction.

First, a word or two about those lesser works of the twenties. *The Man Who Knew Coolidge* is a minor tour de force. Expanded from a magazine piece to book-length during the composition of *Dodsworth*, it consists of six exterior monologues—spoken streams of semiconsciousness full of smug platitudes and self-contradictions, glutting digressions and hypocritical humbug—in which "Lowell Schmaltz, Constructive and Nordic Citizen" freely, proudly, indecently exposes his puny soul. The aim of the book, the exposure of typical middle-class complacency and ignorance and intolerance, is admirable; and if taken in small doses, the author's success at caricaturing a type by no other means than mimicry of speech is impressive. But the book as a whole is too big a dose. Although the speech of Lowell Schmaltz rings true, his fictive long-windedness becomes as wearing to read as it would be to hear in real life. *The Man Who Knew Coolidge* is worth pausing over here just long enough to remark how Schmaltz differs from Lewis' more thoroughly successful principal characters. While he is representative of a type who crops up time and again in the better works—all surface and endless gab, and finally a mere gimmick for satiric illustration—he does not represent the limit of the novelist's ability to create vital characters.

The hero of *Mantrap* is a very un-Schmaltzian figure, but it is doubtful that he can be called a vital character. For *Mantrap* is yet a purer example of the prolific writer's peril, the lapse that has value only as it sheds light on some of the author's abiding preoccupations. Lewis was always fascinated with the attraction of opposites in such friendships as that of Dodsworth and Tub Pearson (a more tolerable version of Lowell Schmaltz), Arrowsmith and the amiable bumpkin Clif Clawson or, later, the intellectual semi-Clawson, Terry Wickett. In *Mantrap*, Ralph Prescott starts out on a roughing-it trip into the wilds of Canada with boisterous Wes Woodbury, but is soon rescued from his intolerable company by Joe Easter, a strong, silent, heart-of-gold woodsman type. One gets the feeling that Lewis, having shown his awareness of pragmatic limits to the unlikeness of companions, would like to see the Ralph-Joe relationship endure; however, his principle of reality prevails. The novel ends with recognition that the ideal fellowship could not hold up in the reality of New York, a reality crueler in its way—in its social stratification, for instance—than the primordial hardness of life at a Canadian outpost.

The novel includes a similar conclusion to another of Lewis' recurring motifs, the marriage of opposites. In many of the early novels—and fully persuasively in *Main Street*— Lewis had paralleled his ideal friendships with a disparate husband-wife team. Joe Easter's wife Alverna is almost as good-natured as he, but she is flighty and flirtatious, in sharp contrast to his steady, phlegmatic character; the marriage naturally fails, as had that of Arrowsmith and his second wife Joyce and as would that of Dodsworth and the Alverna-like Fran. In all these cases of conjoined contraries, both friends and married couples, Lewis seems to have been trying (however consciously—at times the effort looks pretty desperate) to find some way out of a fundamental human dilemma: the deep need to escape loneliness and the difficulties of satisfactory togetherness because of the manifold *difference* of human individuals. In *Mantrap* he comments overtly on this problem of solipsism, noting, for example, that Ralph "perceived how necessary authentic friendship had become to him in a world left vacuous and bewildering by the death of his mother."

The isolation of the individual brings to mind one further aspect of *Mantrap* worth mentioning, its treatment of the "wilderness theme." The wilderness theme is the native American version of pastoral romance, entailing an escape or ameliorative visit to a sort of anti-civilization, a locus of elemental simplicities. Thus Huck Finn lights out for the territory, Thoreau retires for a while to Walden to front the essential facts of life, Ishmael goes to sea, and the Hemingway hero fishes or hunts; Frost, not without ironic ambiguity, instructs the reader of "Directive" how to get back to the wellsprings whose waters may make him whole again. The range extends at least from Natty Bumppo to the weekend campers who descend like locusts on our national forests. Babbitt is able to gain some temporary refreshment from a wilderness vacation, and Arrowsmith must finally retreat to a Waldenic situation in order to quest for his grail of scientific truth free of the hobbles of hyperorganized society. Both, significantly, go with ideal companions: Paul Riesling and Terry Wickett, who embody latent or suppressed parts of the heroes' characters, Babbitt's submerged sensitivity and the inevitable antisocial element of Arrowsmith's intellectual dedication.

Viewed so analytically, these flights from civilization may appear to validate some critics' complaints of a tendency toward escapism in Lewis' work and, still worse, of a too easy, unwitting solution to either the character's problem or the author's problem of characterization, through the happy accident of a sociable alter ego. To my mind, the "escapes" in Lewis' best work are consciously apprehended and artistically apt. But he must have realized that he could not continue to work successful variations on the retreat to the woods with a complementary pal. *Mantrap*, seen from this wide angle, may be considered a testing and partly a purging action, a salutary working out of old themes by bringing them baldly to the fore. The Canadian wilds of *Mantrap* are much the most primitive of Lewis' wildernesses, Ralph is the tenderest of tenderfeet, and the extremity of the situation demands a skeptical handling of the formerly serviceable myth. The hero's meager increase of wisdom at the end shows mainly how foolish he was at the beginning. Spared the onerous companionship of Wes, he must also do without the stalwart Joe, as Joe must do without his mercurial Alverna. Where before Lewis tried to demonstrate a lasting fusion of the opposites that attract, here he has apparently reached the conclusion that the twain can never permanently meet. Ralph is sensibly pleased to be returning to the comforts of his middle-class milieu. Nevertheless, however honest it may be in its representation of general human possibilities, the novel flops. The coy punning of the title, signifying at once a geographical location, the perils of Alvernan attractions, and the self-ensnarement of men who do not know how to leave well enough alone, is a sufficient index to the quality of fiction in *Mantrap*. Students of Lewis may be grateful for the incidental values of a failure; others may wish that the author had worked out his problems in private or had patiently worked them into a living novel.

Mantrap in retrospect looks like a makeshift way-station between *Arrowsmith* and *Elmer Gantry*, the two most dissimilar of the major works. Whereas Gantry is the most detestable of Lewis' protagonists, a mendacious wolf in pastoral clothing, Martin Arrowsmith is the most nearly heroic, the most gifted. Typical in his proclivity for "questing and adventure," Arrowsmith is atypical in his capacity to perform significant service. Lewis begins his story with the expectable sketching in of Arrowsmith's American background, complete with a set of pioneering grand-parents and, later, a Middle Western state university called a "Ford Motor Factory" for its adherence to the modern scheme of mass-production standardization. The university experience anticipates but hardly provides an adequate preparation for the perplexities that Martin continually encounters as he quests his way upward through mazy varieties of commercialism in medicine and science. When he finally becomes a respected part of an affluent scientific foundation, he still finds the path to truth blocked by the demands of institutional *Realpolitik* and the same old tendency toward glossy standardization. So he constrains himself to forego the amenities of success, lighting out for Terry Wickett's territorial retreat.

To outline his progress thus may give the false impression that Arrowsmith is a perfect paragon and that the novel is strictly an attack on contemporary mores using a saintly victim for its weapon. The impressiveness of the novel stems largely from its continuing to function on two distinct though effectively interrelated levels, the social and the personal. The ups and downs of Arrowsmith's career result as much from difficulties of man-against-himself as from those of man-against-society. When Lewis remarks that his protagonist is "in no degree a hero," he refers primarily to the fact that Arrowsmith has his share of human imperfections. His falterings are often of his own making, and when he botches the chance to make a definitive test of the value of his bacteriophage, the cause is his own choice made on the basis of humane emotional considerations instead of the purely intellectual integrity he had hoped to attain—Lewis carefully declines to treat the issues as if they were easy to resolve. Moreover, though he undergoes such serious pathos as the death of his first wife, the obstacles that thwart Arrowsmith are often petty almost to the point of being ridiculous, as if to say that straitened American idealism cannot claim even so much as significantly tragic circumstances. Arrowsmith knows at the end that his shared Walden affords no guarantee of success in his scientific questing, and he experiences considerable regret over having to give up the advantages that his position at the institute and his second, wealthy wife have made available. A measure of Lewis' own progress can be found in his treatment of marital love: the term "playmate" recurs in *Arrowsmith*, but pejoratively. Martin's first wife, Leora, generally regarded as Lewis' best female character, is far more than a jolly partner in youthful gambols; she is quietly resourceful and reliable, sage in the processes of "what every woman knows," devoid of the glamour that distinguishes Joyce, her successor. Martin's necessary rejection of Joyce is signaled by his saying, "You want a playmate, and I want to work." *Arrowsmith* is in part a social novel. It is not farfetched to interpret Martin's experience as representative of the fate of idealism and the disinterested search for truth in twentieth-century America, but the novel never insists on being read symbolically. While it may occasionally grab the reader's lapels, *Arrowsmith* is by and large a deft achievement in fictional rhetoric that persuades rather than harangues.

In the *Saturday Review* of January 28, 1933, Bernard De Voto argued that Lewis was not a realist but a satirist, not really a man with a mimetic gift but an ardent hater with a facility for caricature—a former radical optimist gone sour and lashing out. Applied to the whole of Lewis' work, this judgment is invalid, but it applies with adequate precision to *Elmer Gantry*. Lacking the subtlety and involution of Swift's best work, *Elmer Gantry* is Lewis' most "Swiftian" novel in the sense that it is primarily and relentlessly satiric. Not all the parts of the novel are as hard and heavy as the whole of it seems in retrospect, as indeed it *is* in its over-all effect. The sociological territory of the novel fits in with Lewis' cumulative gazetteer, his charting of American experience in small towns and cities, various sections of the country, and various occupations. It is not unreasonable that the range from aviation to medical science to hotel-keeping should include detailed examination of organized evangelicalism, the new "religious" vaudeville, and the spreading of its materialistic values into the churches. *Elmer Gantry* is, nonetheless, uncharacteristic. The title character is a villain, with none of the saving graces or extenuating circumstances that warrant some sympathy for each of the other protagonists except Lowell Schmaltz, and the relatively harmless Schmaltz was not so much a protagonist as a device. Elmer Gantry is a vital character. If we abstract a list of all his traits and deeds, we may think him melodramatically incredible; yet in the experience of reading the novel we cannot, much as we would like to, deny that he is powerfully alive, full of drive and animal cunning, capable of forceful influence, and very frightening.

It is surprising—or is it?—that this most single-minded, sledge-hammery of the major works should have received perhaps the most expert critical attention. Joseph Wood Krutch was one of the first to note that the sledge-hammer drive of the book did not preclude architectural design: "*Elmer Gantry*, with its innumerable incidents and its many ramifications, is indeed a structure far more impressive than most satires, a sort of cathedral in which every stone is a gargoyle." Rebecca West noted that Gantry was a fully realized creature, a triumph of Lewis' "power of impersonation." Rebecca West, however, did not approve of the book. She found Lewis' own conception of religion little better than Gantry's, and she concluded that the novel was a failure because the novelist was not sufficiently refined and sensitive and intellectually profound. *Elmer Gantry* does fail on these grounds, but they are not its grounds. Sinclair Lewis was not capable of the kind of intellectual art that the critic called for; as she herself in effect acknowledged, when Lewis strove for intellectual profundity he achieved intellectual pretension. Other critics have pointed out that a satirist qua satirist need not explain how to remedy all the evils he blasts: While we may hope that a finer structure will arise where a faulty one has fallen, we do not reasonably require that the demolition expert do the building. Miss West laments that Lewis does not totally dissociate himself from the world of Babbitt by "practising a finer and more complicated mode of thought and feeling," but even if it be assumed that Babbitt is as irremediably execrable (or, stranger yet, as capable of writing the novel that bears his name) as she implies, it is worth remarking that a novelist so exquisitely remote from the workaday world could hardly expect to communicate with the workers. When Miss West objects to specific verbal inelegances and vulgar sentiments in *Elmer Gantry*, failing to appreciate that much of the unitary force of the book derives from the author's deliberate, persistent appropriation of a Gantryan point of view, she at least demonstrates the book's insidious power to arouse the reader, to provoke an emotional reaction. Devised, as Mark Schorer has explained, by the polemical "method of half-truths," *Elmer Gantry* is a book that one can rationally dismiss or discount —it does not convince us, as Lewis surely never intended, that all organized religion is as corrupt as Gantry's brand— but it is not a book easily forgotten. Lewis would have been pleased that some of its mordant energy was able to survive in the prettified technicolor "adaptation" made in Hollywood. And it seems to me that many of the objections raised against the book have been predicated on a categorical sense of what the term "novel" can signify. Very well, then, call it satire; the shifting of labels defuses most of the objections and does nothing to diminish the stature of the author.

If *Mantrap* served as a preparation for the asperity of *Elmer Gantry* by allowing the author to straighten out some of the kinks in his sentimental preferences, *The Man Who Knew Coolidge* may have helped to clear the way for *Dodsworth* by venting the Lewis spleen at many forms of American humbug. For *Dodsworth* is the mellowest of the major works. The hero is as sympathetic though not so potentially significant a character as Arrowsmith, and the portrayal of Dodsworth is seldom if ever distorted by a diversionary jab at phenomena of no special relevance to the progress of the plot. Of course sociological reflections arise: Dodsworth finds himself at loose ends because the day of "bigness" has arrived, vanquishing the possibility of a company president's continuing to operate as a craftsman; he finds the big bank, impressive in its cathedral-like quarters, perplexingly impersonal and indifferent (one thinks of the remote, ontologically independent banks that force people off their land in *The Grapes of Wrath*); there is a passage on the new religion of speed that recalls the theorizing of Henry Adams. As with other of Lewis' heroes, it is possible to read Dodsworth's story as prototypal. The point is, the sociological elements neither insist on primacy nor take the form of obtrusive jeremiads. Oddly enough, a predecessor that *Dodsworth* calls to mind is Henry James. The novel has a kind of Jamesian quietness, an unhurried way of proceeding and a confident forebearance of pointing morals, which must have played a large part in Ford Madox Ford's high estimation of it. Lewis never achieves—he sensibly refrains from trying—James's elegance and mastery of delicate nuance. Such excellences as the delineation of Sam Dodsworth and of Fran, his culturally ambitious, subtly bitchy vampire of a wife—such accomplishments are more straightforward and perhaps less reverberative than James's portraits. All the same, *Dodsworth* generates an atmosphere of ripe, humane discernment quite distinct from the earthy clamor of *Elmer Gantry*. Lewis had a sizable stock of limitations, but he also had more range than the usual summary comment on his work allows.

Readers who thought at the time that the mellowness of *Dodsworth* represented a kind of settling down of Lewis' powers should have known better. He had always taken pains to avoid repeating himself, and though we can now find abundant continuities among his novels, when each originally appeared it came upon the scene with an individual presence noticeably different from that of its fellows. *Ann Vickers* (1933) kept up the pattern of difference. It was more like *Dodsworth*—really more like a combination of *The Job* and *Arrowsmith*—than *Elmer Gantry*, but it was also very different. Typically, Lewis had taken up a whole new area of interest, the conditions and management of prisons. Sex is treated more openly than in previous novels (in *Elmer Gantry* it had necessarily been treated more brutally). A few reviewers thought this first post–Nobel Prize novel showed a real advancement, a further maturing of Lewis' abilities. Nowadays, scarcely anyone would maintain that the later works came up to the quality of the five novels that earned him the prize. He would stick to his task of anatomizing the nation: a hotel novel, an anti-Fascist novel, a theater novel, a novel—as always, in the vanguard, before it became voguish to treat the issue—on the "racial question," and so forth. Lewis had begun to publish at a time when every writer dreamed of producing The Great American Novel. It was a mad dream. However surprisingly close a Dos Passos or a Fitzgerald may have come to creating *a* great American novel, and however gamely Lewis himself may have sometimes courted the vision, he had sense enough to recognize the madness of dreaming that one book could encompass all that welter of diversity; so he tried instead to write a great set of American novels. And he did; at any rate, well enough to merit comparison with Balzac: If the totality of Lewis' writing falls short of being a definitive human comedy, it does add up to a significant American comedy.

But we must admit that after *Dodsworth* the contributions to this cumulative work are, in varying degrees, inferior to Lewis' best. Why he went into decline may never be adequately explained, though partial explanations have been offered. E. M. Forster, arguing that the essential nature of Lewis' accomplishment was "photographic," a sort of quick spontaneous reproduction, speculated that the later work was bound to be lesser because "photography is a pursuit for the young"; when the spontaneity is exhausted, the work will appear to be superficial self-imitation. Others have argued that the American public, in part ironically owing to the success of Lewis' instructive crusading, outgrew the mentor who once set it on its ears. Still other, more superstitious commentators have viewed the prize as an albatross around the laureate's neck, as though Lewis might have gone on to write other works equal or maybe superior to his five best if only the Swedish Academy had waited a few years before canonizing him. Surely there is truth in the argument that the reading public marched ahead while Lewis more or less stood still, but this is an explanation that does not satisfy the question at hand, which is *why* Lewis stood still. He had not stood still on the road that led from *Our Mr. Wrenn* to his great decade. Is it simply that the work of the twenties drained the better part of his creative energy? I do not know. I know that Lewis was not the first writer who continued to write long after he had written his best. And I know that when an artist ages and his powers flag, critical fairness requires that we judge him as he was in his prime.

Toward the end of *L'Alouette*, when the earthly fortunes of Joan of Arc are at their lowest, Anouilh defies the course of history, insisting that a hero deserves to be remembered at his moment of glory, and the play ends with Joan triumphantly present at the coronation of her Charles. It is in this spirit that I have saved Lewis' securest masterpiece, *Babbitt*, for the last in my cursory survey of the novels. I would be willing to argue that *Babbitt* alone was enough to justify the Academy's choice, but I have room for neither argument nor analysis here. A few words of praise will have to suffice. With the possible exception of its "loose" structure, *Babbitt* shows Lewis doing best the things that he could do well. His reportorial eye was so keen that his description of mores, fads and fashions, indicative physical surroundings, and the minutiae of daily life could serve as a time capsule buried to satisfy the curiosity of future centuries. We see the inside and outside of the Babbitts' house with excruciating clarity, and a deceptively simple list of the items in Babbitt's pocket reveals his way of life, his system of values. The novel abounds in the mature Lewisian irony, that peculiar ability to present at once the romantic surface of new phenomena and the befouled underside that seems always to threaten danger of fatal infection. Take, for example, the introductory section: Opening with an almost rhapsodic image of the grandeur of the modern city, Lewis offers a very effective word-painting of Zenith with only an occasional, slight suggestion that the reality beneath the imposing image is sordid or at least unhappy ("a city built—it seemed—for giants"); then comes the central portrait, with a transition discreetly devastating, "There was nothing of the giant in the aspect of the man who was beginning to awaken on the sleeping-porch of a Dutch Colonial house . . . ."

There was nothing of the giant. Somehow, George Babbitt has been plucked from the pages of his fictive life and boiled down to a mere byword, as if Lewis had written "there was nothing of the man." The name "Babbitt" has suffered a lexical sea-change to something admittedly strange enough but too poor to do justice to the novel that branded the name on the modern consciousness. This popular abstraction might be viewed as a testimony to Lewis' stature; "Hamlet" is another name freely wielded by many who have never read the work it comes from; "Robinson

Crusoe" is another; "Tom Sawyer"; the adjectival forms, "Gargantuan," "Quixotic," "Pickwickian." Perhaps any writer who captures the imagination of a wide audience is obliged to find himself more captive than conquerer. However that may be, "Babbittry" is a sneer word that bears only a family resemblance to the sad and funny, poignantly complex simple man whose fumbling life Lewis created with rare insight. Like many of Lewis' protagonists, George Babbitt is a carefully, instrumentally distorted version of the author's self. He is a well-meaning, clubbable but far from perfect man, internally torn between a troubled, barely understood craving for romance or spiritual nourishment and the ever impinging demands of pragmatic reality: there he lies on his sleeping porch, teetering helplessly between his escapist dream and the commanding call of his expensive, mass-produced alarm clock. It was a special gift of Lewis' (Dodsworth is another distinct example) to reveal without fanfare the secret, inchoate life within, the thin dreamer struggling to get out of the fat conformist that encases him; Lewis knew that no Babbitt is all Babbittry, and this is why his major types are never merely types. *Babbitt* contains other varieties of Lewisian excellence: the hilarious spates of plain-folks "booster" talk; the sharply perceived submission to the ineffable potency of status symbols; the "reported" dialogue which, without apparent pointing or authorial comment, convicts the speaker of the crime he disclaims ("Now, I haven't got one particle of race-prejudice"); the forcible descriptive rhetoric of droning repetition, which indicates that Lewis' is fundamentally an oral or tall-story form of humor. All these are inventions and devices that enabled him to illustrate with unrivaled

49

effectiveness the American life of, not quiet, but noisy desperation.

I began this essay by noting that there were overt and timely reasons for Lewis' receiving the prize in 1930, some of them reasons that may strike us as a little too seasonable, a little too much in the nature of ulterior motives. Believing that our main concern today is not so much whether the Swedish Academy's choice was explicable or "inevitable," but whether the choice was good, I have tried to suggest lines of approach to Lewis' work that may help to justify his inclusion among Nobel laureates according to permanent principles; which is to say, on the basis of literary credentials unbounded by considerations of international history, intercultural understanding, or the vicissitudes of taste. But taste does change, and the term "literary" has acquired a restrictedness that some would interpret to exclude Lewis. He had not the exquisite aesthetic sensibility of Henry James, the recondite intellectuality of T. S. Eliot, O'Neill's experimental interest in form, Faulkner's infectious compulsion to grope through metaphysical thickets. The works of many other American writers lend themselves more easily to the current techniques of literary criticism, and thus people who admire Lewis think it best to hail him as an important national happening. His works will endure, they say, but not precisely as "literature." Again we should be willing to concede an argument over terminology. Let us hold on to Lewis' achievement as something other than literary—so long as we acknowledge that the novels can still please us, tickle and prod and test us, instruct us in ways not exclusively sociological.

I have, for obvious reasons, laid heavy stress on the

American qualities of Lewis' writing. I assume it is clear that enlightened literary nationalism has little or nothing to do with a jingoistic sense of what matters; Lewis was manifestly above suspicion of complacent patriotism. Yet there are dangers in stressing his Americanness, above all, the danger of slighting his universal values. No modern nation can afford to overlook an entertaining novelist's weighing against desirable possibilities the sad or ludicrous realities of contemporary experience. But even Lewis' contemporaneity may be overstressed. Although he himself thought such contemporary British realists as H. G. Wells were his true fellows, it has seemed to many readers that the writer Lewis most resembles is Dickens. He had the Dickensian gift for caricature, the Dickensian ability to create extraordinarily memorable characters. Like Dickens, he excelled at scenes of comic melodrama, and he could portray children without the faintest note of adult condescension. Both writers ferociously attacked national institutions, yet did so in such a way that they were appreciated by the very sorts they upbraided (partly because they had that characteristic Lewis attributed to Ann Vickers, "the curst blessing of being able to see the other person's side even when . . . fighting him"); they themselves became national institutions. While they were rebels with heartfelt causes, neither was really a "proletarian writer," dealing primarily with working-class people, or a "revolutionary writer," advocating specific institutional reforms or the wholesale overthrow of the existing social framework. Their criticism of society was fundamentally moral, which explains the absence from their work—though it may not excuse to those who bewail the absence—of concrete constructive suggestion. Lewis had favorable things to say about socialist principles, but,

51

like Dickens, he was in effect a socialist of the heart, what nowadays is apt to be called a sentimental liberal. Lewis was, in other words, an imaginative moralist, and it is unlikely that the perfection of human nature will soon make his moralizing obsolete. It may not be particularly fashionable now for novelists to care first and foremost about people, but Lewis did care, and the fact that in his best work his sense of reality held his caring short of sentimentality bolsters my confidence that his work will endure.

My epigraph is taken from Lewis' hotel novel, *Work of Art*, a book that does not live up to its title. Were we to judge the writer by such lesser works, we might indulge in a snide application of the epigraph to his writings: complete, yes; but crude. Lewis was not a "stylist," which usually means one who manipulates the language in a strikingly elegant way; nor did he fashion for himself, writing in his own voice, a peculiar and only apparently imitable idiom like Hemingway's or Faulkner's. Yet he did manage gradually to develop a perfectly serviceable plain style that could be put to a variety of uses. Sometimes he could, as his Nobel acceptance speech and some of the better descriptive passages in *Babbitt* illustrate, write notably vivid prose; but the grand style was not his forte, and usually when he reached for beauties, they exceeded his grasp. Furthermore, for all his admirable pioneering in the removal of the "American Fear of Literature" (the title of his acceptance speech), he added no significant new dimensions to the form of the novel. It would not be grossly unfair to say that he poured his twentieth-century wines into nineteenth-century bottles. We must remember, however, that the immortalization of crude fact is not itself a crude or an easy triumph. In time more innovative and intellectual

American authors would travel to Stockholm the trail that Sinclair Lewis had blazed. Meanwhile, there was the pioneer in spats, radiantly grateful, surprisingly modest and self-effacing, awkwardly but ineluctably immortal.

EUGENE O'NEILL

by Jordan Y. Miller

Wᴴᴱɴ ᴇᴜɢᴇɴᴇ ᴏ'ɴᴇɪʟʟ was awarded the Nobel Prize for 1936, there were those, including O'Neill himself, who expressed surprise at the choice of another American so soon after Sinclair Lewis. For the most part, the award was greeted with enthusiasm, both in America and abroad, particularly among the professional critics who had closely followed O'Neill's twenty-year rise to prominence and who felt that the selection provided a justified world recognition of the international leadership that American drama had now gained, primarily through O'Neill's efforts. Some who deplored the choice argued that O'Neill's creation of effective showpieces did not necessarily constitute great literary achievement, but their voices remained a minority. (Among the strongest of the opposition was Bernard De-Voto, who expressed his dismay in "Minority Report," *Saturday Review of Literature*, November 21, 1936. The anonymous author of "Counsels of Despair," appearing in *The Times Literary Supplement* of April 10, 1948, found, even after twelve years, that the award had been "capricious." Brooks Atkinson in "Ennobel-ing O'Neill," *New York Times* Theatre Section, November 22, 1936, spoke effectively for the affirmative.)

The prizes could not have gone to two more different writers than O'Neill and Lewis. Their literary media and their thematic approaches were wholly unlike. Lewis was a writer of fiction, and his award acknowledged the position of American novelists as equals among world peers. With the award to O'Neill, however, the prize went to one who practiced an American art form that had only within the two decades of O'Neill's career been recognized as worthy of any serious consideration. Moreover, the designation fell upon a man who wrote nothing whatever but plays. O'Neill was purely and simply a dramatist who chose, with rarest exception, to work exclusively in this medium throughout his entire productive life. The tragic temperament of O'Neill's artistry bore little semblance to Lewis' satiric social exposés. O'Neill's social awareness was confined to a genuine concern for what happened to men's souls in a tragic world; the ills and evils of society as a whole were not his to argue. In a widely quoted statement he once explained his outlook by saying, "Most modern plays are concerned with the relation between man and man, but that does not interest me at all. I am interested only in the relation between man and God." This was an attitude unique in the stage literature of his time and, combined with O'Neill's underlying mysticism, was remarkably uncommon in the rest of the literature of the age.

Furthermore, this prize winner was a man who never became permanently identified with any established artistic movement. O'Neill exerted no direct influence upon, nor did he form around him, any literary school. Throughout his life he remained an independent creative force, refusing to be guided by pre-existing attitudes. In any given sequence of plays he could employ the most diametrically opposed techniques, while consistently violating every established procedure of contemporary dramaturgy, but in doing so, he took himself and his work completely seriously and expected his public to do the same. He was determined to keep his plays above the level of the commercial show shop and to remain consistent with his own statement made in his 1914 application for admission to George Pierce Baker's Harvard playwriting class: "I want to be an artist or nothing."

O'Neill had just published his first slim book of plays, entitled *Thirst and Other One-Act Plays*, which was a failure in all ways, financial and artistic. In that year of 1914, if one were to seek among the younger American writers for a potential winner of any form of literary prize, he would not have found the Eugene O'Neill name on any conceivable list. There could hardly have been a candidate of less promise, for O'Neill at twenty-six offered a casebook example of the complete failure. He had never held a steady job in his life. He had left college (Princeton) without even completing his freshman year, had worked erratically as a seaman on a variety of Atlantic vessels, had lived as a destitute wharf bum in South America, very nearly turning to crime to survive, and had existed on a minuscule dole from his father in waterfront bars and flea-bag rooming houses in New York. At twenty, almost on a dare, he had married a girl he hardly knew, fathered a child he never saw until nearly twelve years later, went gold prospecting in Honduras, contracted malaria, and was divorced before he was twenty-two. He failed as a newspaper reporter, be-

came intimate with all the more infamous New York and
Connecticut bordellos, to which he was guided by his
brother, James; evidenced all the symptoms of fast becoming a hopeless alcoholic; and, after attempting suicide, contracted a severe enough lung infection to place him in a
Connecticut tuberculosis sanitorium for six months at the
age of twenty-four. His father, the widely known romantic
actor, James O'Neill, totally despaired of his son's future
and all but gave him up as a derelict wastrel, broken in
health and utterly dependent upon parental generosity to
keep alive.

What no outsider could possibly have realized was that,
amid the apparent wreckage of a young life, there existed
a lonely, sensitive, artistic spirit denied any form of expressive outlet in the unsettled home of a parsimonious
father, a morphine-addicted mother, and a totally dissipated brother. The wild, aimless living was but a protest,
a desperate search for escape, that only succeeded in further
sublimating the incipient artist who, by O'Neill's own admission, envied the freedom of the sea gulls that soared
around him on deck watch as he sailed aboard a square-
rigged schooner. Finally, with the apparently doomed man
incapacitated by illness and held inactive by long months
of recuperation, the underlying force of the artist began to
assert itself. It would be years before the alcoholism was
overcome, and two more marriages were ahead. Even then,
the continual wandering in search of a permanent and satisfactory home for the restless soul would never cease.

But the immediate point is that, at the age of twenty-six,
the convalescent O'Neill had discovered what he wanted to
do. He wanted to write plays. Confident that he had something to offer, he refused to be discouraged as manuscript

after manuscript returned without comment from the New York producers to whom he sent them. By the time he was introduced into the midst of the small band of intellectuals summering in Provincetown in 1916, who were willing to stage some of the contents of the "trunk of unproduced one-act plays" that supposedly accompanied him, he was prepared to present the proof that he was determined, indeed, to be an artist or nothing.

The Nobel citation never mentions a specific item as the *raison d'être* of the award, choosing rather to let the awardee's body of works stand as evidence of meritorious accomplishment. O'Neill's cumulative output is impressive, for he had written well over fifty plays in the slightly more than twenty years before 1936. Although the total drops sharply when the twenty-odd unpublished or unacted pieces of his very early period are eliminated, there remains the still substantial figure of thirty-four commercially produced new plays from 1916 to 1934, a total no recent American playwright has even remotely approached.

But quality, not quantity, is the ultimate criterion, an aspect even more remarkable in O'Neill's case than mere numbers. Within those thirty-four plays are some of the most memorable characters and overpowering theatrical experiences in modern American drama; on the other hand, there is also exhibited some of the dullest, most inept blather ever written for the stage. There was never a middle ground, an "average" O'Neill play. It either soared, or it plummeted. The Nobel committee, however, looking beyond the limits of any single creation, was able to view the whole of the existing canon with a dispassionate approach generally denied the domestic critic forced to witness the piecemeal accumulation of an erratic body of literature.

The committee seems to have followed closely the reasoning of Joseph Wood Krutch, who saw the pattern of O'Neill's development as early as 1924. Writing in *The Nation* (November 26, 1924), he said, "The meaning and unity of his work lies not in any controlling intellectual idea and certainly not in a 'message,' but merely in the fact that each play is an experience of extraordinary intensity."

If Eugene O'Neill had written nothing else, he would stand as one of the great composers of one-act plays. He regarded this abbreviated form of drama as something far more than amusing skit or simple sketch, holding it quite capable of theatrical impact every bit as strong as any longer, "full-length" creation. From the beginning, even in 1913 and 1914, he infused his short plays with the strong intensity of feeling that he would constantly display throughout his career, and he was publicly accepted as a serious writer from the start. In 1919, within three years of his first production, he had established himself as the most important writer of one-act plays in the contemporary American theater. Twelve had already been staged and seven were in print in a rapidly selling published version, *Moon of the Caribbees and Six Other Plays of the Sea.*

The seven plays of this first successful O'Neill anthology are the best of his entire one-act collection. (Only two others are worth consideration, *Before Breakfast* and *The Dreamy Kid*, both second rate.) *Bound East for Cardiff*, produced at the Wharf Theatre in Provincetown during the summer of 1916, was the first to be written and produced, and probably the best of the lot, demonstrating how well O'Neill eschewed all the tricks of many an established one-act playwright. In the normally accepted sense of the word, it is scarcely a play at all. There is no plot, there is no

59

action. The characters are quickly established as easily recognizable types, speaking convincing if stagey, national dialects, and they develop no further. Conflict is non-existent; a crisis or climax fails to materialize. All that transpires is the slow death of a fatally injured sailor lying delirious in his bunk as his shipmates pursue their assigned duties in a driving rainstorm, and the dying man's closest friend clumsily attempts to solace him. Except for the moment of death itself, nothing whatever occurs. The impact is delivered through O'Neill's intimate knowledge of what such men might logically say and do in this situation, and he has recreated an almost unbearable intensity concentrated on the stricken man's agony and the inability of his companions to do a thing to help him. By most standards of the time the play should have failed miserably. Instead, when the curtain closed on the first performance, the audience sat silent and deeply moved at this display of pain, fear, sorrow, and hopeless helplessness, conveyed with authority by one who knew and caught the essence of all such brief moments in man's existence.

The remaining plays vary widely in subject matter and emphasis. Although *The Moon of the Caribbees* and *The Dreamy Kid* continue in the tradition of *Cardiff*, exploring a situation rather than developing action or character, the melodramatics of *In the Zone* and *The Long Voyage Home* and the psychotic, monomaniac figures of *Ile*, *Where the Cross Is Made*, and *The Rope* provide acceptable and interesting variety. Even the tour de force of the monologue which forms the entirety of *Before Breakfast* cannot be dismissed without a realization of its horrifying hypnotic attraction. The most important strength of these brief dramas is their tremendous sense of mood combined with authenticity of atmosphere, whether set in the forecastle of a plodding tramp steamer or ashore in the house of a mad old captain. Each is uniformly in the firmest tradition of stage realism, with character, situation, and theme constantly suggesting the grimly detailed revelations of literary naturalism. Beyond that, they are plays that cannot be quickly thrown together for hasty production; they demand great skill from director and actor alike. Their themes of man's frustrations, isolation, indifference, and callous brutality, displayed within a framework of genuine sympathy for and understanding of humanity, cannot casually be portrayed. Of great significance, as well, is their demonstration of O'Neill's unerring intuitive awareness of *theater*, an artistic advantage that, in the future, would carry to success many of his far more difficult and thematically obtuse endeavors. They stand as important today as when they were written, and in no small way they represent a microcosm of all of O'Neill's plays to come.

The years 1920–25 were simultaneously the most unsettled and the most active of O'Neill's career. It is a difficult period to classify because of the variety and unevenness of the output; "shakedown years" might serve as an adequate description. Among the sixteen plays that O'Neill wrote, only five offer any solid basis for his recognition as America's major dramatic power. Fortunately, they appeared among the remaining eleven failures at appropriate enough intervals that complete and obliterating disaster was constantly forestalled, although he drove his well-wishers frantic as they constantly prayed that he would settle down and produce a body of drama displaying some sort of artistic consistency.

This, however, O'Neill was never able to do. The cumulative effect of his erratic production during these five years was something like a wild roller-coaster ride. One was never quite sure how far down the car might plunge nor, on the contrary, how high it might climb, with imminent and fatal derailment a constant threat at either end. But in spite of two Pulitzer Prizes, the depths were too deep and the heights not quite lofty enough. Although the triumphs eventually came to outweigh the disasters, they would have to be coupled with the dramatic giants yet to come to justify anything so significant as a Nobel Prize for literature. To be honest, before 1926, O'Neill was hardly more than a rather daring, though admittedly exciting, experimenter.

At least ten of the sixteen plays from 1920 to 1925 were in the tradition of the stage realism that had been O'Neill's earlier hallmark of success. As an avowed Strindbergian, he also made heavy use of the war between the sexes, analyzing and dissecting his characters against the sordid background atmosphere and somber moods so typical of the Swedish naturalist. Unlike other American "realists" such as Clyde Fitch, Edward Sheldon, Eugene Walter, or even David Belasco, all of whom tended toward melodramatics and purely moralistic, if not exactly happy, endings, O'Neill showed his growing preference for the tragic theme that was to become so important a few years hence. Nonetheless, during this time he held to no uniform style as he wrote two signal contributions to the development of American stage expressionism, ventured into full-fledged poetic drama, and tried his hand at adaptation.

Beyond the Horizon, the 1920 Pulitzer Prize winner, must be regarded as an important milestone not only for O'Neill but for modern American drama. It is the first full-length

O'Neill play to be staged anywhere, and his first venture on Broadway beyond the limits of the made-over stables and brownstones in Greenwich Village. It retains the intensity of the earlier plays, while at the same time avoiding any suggestion of "thesis" or "social" problem so often associated with long realistic drama. Instead, it discusses the responsibility of the individual to his own soul and conscience, or God, while its Strindbergian sex battle underlies a near-tragic character struggle. *Beyond the Horizon* is certainly not a wholly realized tragedy, although the elements are there. While the protagonist, Robert Mayo, seems to fall to pieces with no evidence of any tragic struggle or dignity, he does, in his way, face up to the hopeless reality of his situation and achieves an awareness of the flaws within himself that have brought destruction upon the house of Mayo. The ultimate catastrophe descends with a certain amount of inevitability, although the return to tranquility in the ultimate working out of the disaster is not strongly affirmed. But, tragic or not, the play brought public and critic to the jolting recognition that the spiritual and physical decay of a young man living in contemporary society, violating his own moral principles, doomed to a slow disintegration in body and spirit, was fit subject for absorbing theater. In the words of Alexander Woollcott, summarizing typical critical reaction in the *New York Times* (February 4, 1920), the play contained so much meat that it made all other current offerings "seem like so much meringue."

After the withdrawal of *Chris* following its failure in Atlantic City and the single appearance of the one-act *Exorcism* in Greenwich Village, both performed in March, 1920, and both heavily realistic, O'Neill executed an abrupt about-face in style, which left spectators stunned and sent critics into the kind of ecstasy of praise that every playwright dreams of and seldom receives. The theme still dwelt upon the pitiful disintegration of a soul in torment, but the way it was portrayed was something entirely new to the jaded sophisticates who regularly patronized New York theaters. The writer of "stark tragedy" and "sordid realism" now found himself famous literally overnight as a leader of the vanguard of a new movement. The style was expressionism and the play was *The Emperor Jones*, the first title that almost invariably comes to mind whenever O'Neill's name is mentioned.

Brutus Jones, the murdering former Pullman porter, is probably the most famous character in American drama, with the possible exceptions of Willie Loman and Blanche Dubois. His terrified flight through the West Indian jungles and his vivid hallucinations became the American prototype of stylized stagecraft. His silver bullets and heart-timed drumbeats became known around the world. However, *The Emperor Jones* today seems greatly overrated. As a piece of genuine expressionism, it has its faults, and as a piece of dramatic literature, it has serious flaws. Except for a certain grotesqueness surrounding Jones's position as "emperor," the play makes little use of the techniques of true expressionism. Its episodic projection of Jones's disintegrating mind are, to be sure, highly inventive and terrifyingly immediate, and they do make use of the theater's mechanical devices to express the panic and turmoil of a doomed creature. These flashbacks, nightmarish as they are, lack the exaggeration and distortion in word, action, and form generally associated with expressionistic staging. Jones, Smithers, and the natives around them, while perhaps greater than life, are still life*like*. The effect of expressionism is abundantly present, but O'Neill's use of the style itself is undeveloped. The play shows O'Neill in full command of his sense of theatricality, but it remains too much a piece of theater and too little a work of dramatic art. With less than superb staging and with anything short of a brilliant performance, the whole affair can turn into a ludicrous bag of tricks. The hallucinations themselves are in constant danger of becoming ridiculous, and the monologue becomes progressively ineffective. Aside from a painfully slow opening scene of highly inferior exposition and a brief conclusion, the play is a one-man tour de force.

As a piece of tragedy, the play falls short, although it remains a fine example of O'Neill's concern for man's relation to his God. Jones has put his Jesus on the shelf and is now forced to face his own soul; a giant man, reduced to bodily and spiritual nakedness as he grovels in the primordial mud. This ultimate catastrophe is ironic, not tragic. Jones is justly punished, and his fall scarcely moves us to the necessary heights of tragic pity.

It would be a full year before O'Neill was able to recapture his audience with a new play that lived up to the promise of *Beyond the Horizon* or *The Emperor Jones*, and another four months beyond that before he abandoned the realism that had once served him so well but that had come close to smothering everything he did. In a series of four plays—*Diff'rent, Gold, The Straw*, and *The First Man*—O'Neill drenched his stage with lunacy, disease, and death. Lacking any of the compensating refinements of sympathetic characters or attractive themes, the plays drove the audiences out of the theater and the critics out of their minds. To look back on the output of this rather desperate period is to be astonished at what O'Neill thought he could force upon his viewers and demand of his actors. Furthermore, the mounting catastrophe of failure after failure could have meant the end for a playwright less determined than O'Neill.

The welcome given the rewritten *Chris*, which opened as *Anna Christie* in November, 1921, proved that for all the sterility of the other four, O'Neill was still capable of handling realistic techniques in a long play. It is true that the protagonist is a prostitute, and there is the continual presaging of doom in old Chris's continual reminder of the devilish sea, but with the alcoholic Marty and the bruising Matt to help, the play emerges as good comedy—humane, amusing, and compassionate. O'Neill's old-time authenticity of believably portrayed waterfront characters and atmosphere is vigorously displayed. The ironies are many and well defined, but they only further the excellence of the dramatic conflict without descending to maudlin melodramatics. In addition, O'Neill has painted one of his most romantic stage pictures. The sea and the fog are cleansing; Anna will find redemption with the help of the burly stoker who comes out of the fog to be nursed back to health by the ministering angel. The conclusion suggests a "happy" ending, but the threat of future trouble, known only to the old devil of a sea, hangs forbiddingly over all. O'Neill never felt that the play was among his best, but his public overruled him. This winner of O'Neill's second Pulitzer Prize remains his best "straight" play in its excellent acting roles and its warm audience appeal.

The Hairy Ape, staged only five days after *The First Man*, brought O'Neill out of the slough of realistic claptrap with a rush that carried him once more into the forefront as America's outstanding theatrical experimenter and straight up to the doors of New York's City Hall. The giant stoker Yank cursed and shouted his way into his place as O'Neill's finest expressionistic creation, while simultaneously bringing down the wrath of New York's suddenly offended guardians of public morality. By today's wide-open standards *The Hairy Ape* is mild indeed. The profanity and the crude vulgarities that shocked the sensibilities of 1922 seem almost childish now. Fortunately, this very exciting play defied and survived the little people who would have closed it. Yank is a beautiful conception of elemental man, confronted with the outside world as decadent as his world of the stokehole is filthy, as empty in meaning as his is lacking in human comforts. He is also a creature without faith, and he cannot survive as long as he remains apart from some identity with the forces beyond him. He is a vigorous expression of O'Neill's favorite theme of the relation of man to God. Also, as an example of theatrical expressionism, *The Hairy Ape* is much better than *The Emperor Jones*. It deserves high recognition as a brilliant piece of stylized drama. The opening scene of the ape-like stokers and their hollow laughter far surpasses the tedium of *Jones's* expository opening dialogue. All of Yank's mounting despair is conveyed through fully realized expressionistic exaggeration and distortion, never quite achieved in *Jones*, and arouses much greater audience compassion than can be offered to the crafty, sinister emperor.

The next year to witness an O'Neill production was 1924. It began ominously. March entertained the opening of the dullest thing O'Neill ever wrote, called *Welded*, a straight-down-the-line Strindbergian battle of the sexes. Its endless talk and nonexistent action enabled it to breathe through twenty-four performances before it died unmourned. April was little better. O'Neill dabbled with expressionistic adaptation, crowding the tiny Provincetown stage with a hybrid product of enacted recitation interpreting Coleridge's *The Ancient Mariner*. All who caught its four-week run knew immediately that O'Neill had reached beyond his element.

In May there was improvement, for then appeared one of O'Neill's most significant plays, the highly controversial and always disappointing *All God's Chillun Got Wings*. It is historically important because it presented a subject so alien to its time as to place once more the forces of law and order on the alert, not for obscenities or indecency, but for the fact that O'Neill dared to have his white heroine kiss the hand of her Negro husband. The wild reaction of City Hall in its attempt to cut off the production before the world exploded indicates how dangerous this almost revolutionary theme of miscegenation seemed to those in power at the time. The mayor's office sought to halt the opening by denying permission to use children in the first scene. The scene was therefore read to the audience from the stage, and the play proceeded, unmolested, as planned, for a respectable run. The play disappoints because of its awkward structure, and there is too much sudden madness, more akin to Elizabethan revenge drama than to a modern social document. The marital battles become grotesque and lack conviction. Yet, *All God's Chillun* very nearly rises above its shortcomings. O'Neill has been able to use a racial problem without actually creating a racial-problem play, for he is once again vitally interested in the man-to-God relationship. Jim—intelligent, gentle, capable—cannot emotionally compete with the white world; Ella—ignorant, crude, vicious—can only contemptuously regard her husband as beneath her. A faith to transcend the forces destroying them is desperately needed, and the ironies of its lack are effectively portrayed.

With the opening of *Desire Under the Elms* in November, 1924, O'Neill found his critics using such terms as "Greek" and "classic" in praising its tragic qualities, although there were those who saw only violent melodrama and monomania inherited from earlier works. The moralists marched once more, as well, with "play juries" formed to pass on the validity of this and other plays as dramatic art. As usual, the threats were empty, and the play entered a long and successful run.

Desire Under the Elms, O'Neill's most positive assertion of his man-to-God theme up to this time, is about as close to genuine tragedy as had yet been created in America. In revival it never fails to display the rugged power of a thoroughly gripping drama of emotional violence. Ephraim Cabot, drawn so much larger than life, emerges as one of O'Neill's strongest figures, a true giant; but for all our reluctant admiration of him, he fails to achieve the heights of tragedy and remains unchanged, as adamant at the end as at the beginning. Eben and Abbie, on the other hand, uncomprehending of the basic natural forces which move them, fiercely seek their rights and pursue with equal fierceness their passions, finally uniting in a tragic realization of their doom. They have, in their way, become redeemed, and as they leave the stage the evil forces that destroyed them are dead; the Cabot farm returns to tranquility. There is a positive and elevating conclusion to this play, despite its horrors of adultery, murder, and suggestions of incest, that gives it the aura of genuine tragedy during its most heightened moments.

One more play, *The Fountain,* in December of 1925,

closed out O'Neill's first decade as a professional play-wright. A poetic jumble of pseudo-historic pageantry, suffocating under a mountain of elegant scenery, it hit the bottom of the O'Neill roller coaster and passed out of sight after twenty-four performances.

By 1926 it would have been difficult indeed to regard O'Neill as anything less than a thoroughly established and successful playwright. It is nevertheless foolish to assume that he could have been seriously considered for anything as important as the Nobel Prize. The discouragingly uneven total output gave no indication that a positive artistry might emerge. He was, of course, acknowledged as a serious, eccentric, possibly brilliant young revolutionary who beat about him on all sides with a rashness that forced everyone in sight to keep a respectable distance, but O'Neill had as yet maintained a more or less traditional manner in his works, however shocking and violent they may have seemed. Most of the plays hewed closely to the realistic line, half of them embarrassingly inept. Even the expressionistic plays, while among the best of their kind, were in a stage tradition already established in Europe, and other Americans, such as Elmer Rice in his excellent *The Adding Machine*, were using the style with skill. O'Neill's preference for the tragic set him apart from others practicing at the time, but there would have to be something more. The next ten years were to provide it.

Over these ten years O'Neill's production of new plays dropped to eight. The roller coaster gave no sign of leveling off, but this was the decade in which appeared the works that, for all the triteness of the word, must be termed monumental. As always, paired against them, were other plays that must bear the label monstrous. It is the period that gave the public a "new" O'Neill as well, the playwright with a sense of humor. It is the time when the writer of near-classic tragedy suddenly seemed to "get religion." It is the time, as well, when world acclaim brought the Nobel Prize.

O'Neill's only new production in 1926, *The Great God Brown*, staged in January, comes very close to being his greatest play. The first introduction to it can be baffling. The profusion of masks can become an exasperating interference with audience comprehension of what is going on, but if they are accepted as a legitimate theatrical device, they can contribute to an absorbing adventure in theatergoing. Their challenge to the imagination does more to stimulate the viewer than any number of literal transcriptions of reality. There are times, one cannot deny, when an audience must extend itself to the utmost in accepting the convention. Near the final curtain, with the masks confused with entire human bodies, the temptation is strong to cry out, "Hold, enough!" In the main, however, O'Neill seems well aware of what he is attempting, and the cumulative effect is enthralling.

The Great God Brown should not be seen as tragedy, but is probably best classified as a modern morality play. Every character, though separate and independent, is at the same time a personification of some aspect of man as a whole. The interplay of the four protagonists, however, still remains intense and gripping in a vivid and exciting drama. Although the device is far from original, O'Neill's use of the masks is unique in contemporary theater. The argument that they cannot adequately convey the several facets of a living changing human being is no more valid than it is to say that Hamlet's soliloquies cannot honestly convey every nuance of that complex character. O'Neill is greatly concerned with the inability of intelligent men and women to establish any line of direct communication, and he is equally concerned with society's consistent refusal to accept the sensitive artist in its midst. The masks, together with his most poetic language, convey his concern better than he had been able to do in all his previous plays. O'Neill's own published explanation, appearing in several newspapers in mid-February, 1926, as "The Playwright Explains," did little to clarify anything further, and it is best to avoid its somewhat befuddled analysis.

The last year in which O'Neill released more than one play was 1928, and it was the first year that the Theatre Guild became his sole producer. The Guild's first production, a luxurious staging of *Marco Millions*, unveiled the most lighthearted O'Neill that audiences had yet seen. Into thirteenth-century Cathay he sent a glad-handing Rotarian-oriented young Marco Polo, whose traveling-salesman skills were to bring the realm of Kublai Khan into the "modern" world of efficient mediocrity and legislated happiness. As the prototype creation of the "ugly American," O'Neill's Polo is amusing, but O'Neill's belated attack on Babbittry was no longer timely and had, moreover, already been done much better by O'Neill's prize-winning predecessor, Sinclair Lewis. *Marco Millions* was a wobbly beginning for the Guild's association with O'Neill, but it was soon forgotten in the midst of the sensation of the next play, the marathon biography of the sex life of Nina Leeds.

Strange Interlude offers the most fascinating character in all of O'Neill's works and, unless one chooses Williams' Blanche Dubois, the most fascinating female in American drama. The hypnotic power of the near-psychotic Nina exhibits the predatory nature of the female far beyond even Strindberg's most vicious jungle beast. Enthusiastic audiences filled the theater night after night, month after month, to watch her cast the spell of her eternal womanhood over father, husband, and lover. The frankness of language and theme, the revelation of innermost thought, gave the illusion of witnessing a public experiment in psychoanalysis, with all the clandestine thrills of overhearing what was never meant to be spoken outside the privacy of the clinic. Nina's obsession with the dead Gordon and her disastrous determination to eliminate her guilt complexes, coupled with her final descent and release into a world of decaying sexlessness, form an unforgettable picture of a woman's potent forces gone terrifyingly awry. When O'Neill places her in tableau amidst her worshipers during the play's high point and she informs the audience of her secure happiness with "my three men," he has created one of his most chillingly memorable scenes.

The critical reception, save in some important instances, was enthusiastic in the extreme. O'Neill was hailed as the hewer of new ways, a cleaver of skylines, a creator of theater compared to which all future plays would pale into insignificance. Such praise has, by now, returned to proper perspective and seems foolishly naïve, for *Strange Interlude* was a solitary achievement, never duplicated with success by O'Neill, nor imitated by others. Still, there can be no question but that its nine acts and six hours struck with tremendous force and surprised an American theater that was by now certain it had become blasé enough about the innovations of this unpredictable writer not to be surprised by anything.

Strange Interlude, for all its power, is not a great play.

The fault does not lie in the soliloquy-asides, although they tend to become irritating and tiresome. Like the masks of *The Great God Brown*, they can be tolerated if their theatrical validity is recognized. Neither does the fault lie in the characterization of Nina. Her behavior may be illogical and often wildly irrational, but it is well documented at any rate. Nor is size alone a fault, even though the play could be cut in half with no loss. Probably the greatest weakness is the lack of conviction. The Freudian implications are too obvious. The supporting characters are too submissive, too "gutless" in the face of Nina's assault. They stand hopelessly childish in their inability to recognize that the obsession with the dead Gordon is, after twenty years, a sign of serious mental disturbance. Mrs. Evans' tale of family insanity is contrived nineteenth-century Gothicism; her subsequent plea for the bearing of an illegitimate child turns grotesquely absurd. The complexes and fixations of "good old Charley" are as tiresome as Nina's obsession. Perhaps most important is the fact that the play lacks a point of view. The audience is deprived of the aesthetic satisfaction expected of good drama. Is *Strange Interlude* a tragedy? Is it an antifeminist tract, or a psychological study of a nymphomaniac? Is it a satire on all amateur analysts and pseudo-Freudian practitioners? Or is it a long, drawn-out sex melodrama? Could it be a probe "in depth" of that elusive something called the "feminine mystique"? Is it some kind of elaborate morality? an extended mystic metaphor? It is, of course, one of O'Neill's strongest assertions of the personal tragedy of loss of soul. Its questioning of the meaning of God, with Nina's statement that God should be a woman, is pertinent and well said. Surely it is more than that, but it remains to the individual spectator to determine what it is.

Today, in revival, *Strange Interlude* can still engross, but one is uncomfortably aware that its ring is now more than a little hollow, its aims disturbingly pretentious. It remains one of O'Neill's most compelling plays, the first of the "monumental" creations. Few who saw it could argue that it deserved yet another Pulitzer Prize.

The mightiest failure of O'Neill's career was *Lazarus Laughed*, "A Play for an Imaginative Theatre." Realizing that no commercial theater would attempt it, O'Neill still regarded it as one of his best creations. The physical demands of the play are, for all practical purposes, impossible. The hundreds upon hundreds of masks conveying the entire spectrum of humanity are a tremendous burden to the producer, who could hardly expect to come anywhere near to the subtleties demanded by O'Neill's complex stage directions. The laughter that Lazarus brings out of the tomb imposes a well-nigh insurmountable difficulty upon any actor. Only two performances, both amateur, were ever undertaken. The Pasadena Community Playhouse did a full-scale production in April, 1928, to a mixed reception. Fordham University students who undertook it in 1948 abandoned the laughter for an unsuccessful sounding of a bell. Ultimately, *Lazarus Laughed* begins to dull the senses while, paradoxically, mounting simultaneously toward hysteria. O'Neill fails here in trying to bring God down to earth as an oversimplified pagan concept, a creature of Dionysiac laughter. Salvation comes through a laughing rejection of the fear of death, but there seems to be little else that O'Neill has to say. The confusion and encumbrances of the technical demands reduce the play to closet drama, a level on which it may achieve some kind of permanent value.

Dynamo in February of 1929 was awaited as the first of a proposed trilogy in which O'Neill was to explore the "death" of the old God and the search for a new one to replace it. The play ranks among the three or four worst things that O'Neill ever created, and the trilogy, needless to say, was never completed. *Dynamo's Strange Interlude* monologues had nothing to offer except poor imitation. Reuben Light is a psychotic protagonist whose worship of electricity turns into a raving madness, depriving him of any of the appeal of *Interlude's* Nina Leeds. The highly effective cutaway house that appeared on stage in *Desire Under the Elms* becomes here an ineffective stage gimmick, and the photographic realism of the powerhouse setting intrudes violently upon the over-all stylization. The message concerning dead and new gods is obliterated by the fixations of Light, who solves all in a spectacular finale of murder and then suicide upon the cathodes of the dynamo. O'Neill insisted this was one of his better efforts and that his message "stood out like red paint," but if that is so, the audiences that supported its brief run were acutely colorblind.

It is probably a good honest guess that the play which most influenced the Nobel committee's 1936 nomination of Eugene O'Neill was the climactic effort of his lifetime career, *Mourning Becomes Electra*. In a world not yet attuned to mid-century "absurdities," O'Neill's trilogy of doom and death in Civil War New England was greeted with almost universal enthusiasm as the dramatic accomplishment of the era.

The first point of importance in evaluating this five-hour

marathon is to ignore the obvious parallels to Aeschylus. Studied too closely, they easily turn into a parody of the original Greek, a matter quite beside the point. The play must be judged on the merits of O'Neill's interpolations and the effect created through his characters and their development of the tragic theme. The most significant change actually makes O'Neill's version more genuinely tragic than the original. The removal of the tragic emphasis from the weak and essentially defenseless Orestes (Orin) to the strong and terrible Electra (Lavinia) totally eliminates the need for a *deus ex machina* rescue of the protagonist. O'Neill's Electra figure welcomes the pursuing Furies who drive her behind the doors of her home into an entombment designed to punish and to expiate the family curse.

O'Neill's is not a Greek world, but an American New England world; the problems are not of the Fates set upon man from the heights of Olympus, but of modern psychology, and yet O'Neill's man-to-God theme is clear. His characters are placed in direct confrontation with the eternal, and they are constantly aware of it. The tragic catastrophe becomes inevitable long before the first play of the trilogy is complete; the struggle against it becomes increasingly terrifying, even grandly so. As Lavinia closes the house in upon herself with unmistakable tragic finality, there is restored to the community the tranquility of a genuinely tragic dénouement.

To attack *Mourning Becomes Electra* on the basis of its lack of elevated poetic diction, or for its ponderous or repetitious nature, is to attack virtually any of O'Neill's important plays. Such an attack is gratuitous, for the play still remains a high-water mark in American theatrical experience. If anyone had previously doubted that O'Neill fully meant to go down as a writer of modern tragedy, *Mourning Becomes Electra* dispelled any such question. O'Neill's combination of high purpose and effective theatricality brought the production not only large audiences for a season but more uniform acclaim than the playwright had ever before received.

The reversal from the heights of Olympus to his "satyr play" *Ah, Wilderness!* was abrupt and complete, taking the serious playgoer completely by surprise. That O'Neill could write a warm domestic comedy, let alone that he even had a sense of humor, was a revelation to all but his most intimate acquaintances. To those few who knew the playwright as a close personal friend, O'Neill's lighter side had often been revealed, but to the public he was always the man who had seen hell. The delight with which this "comedy of recollection" was welcomed marked a new attitude toward O'Neill. The man was, *mirabile dictu*, human after all.

The initial assumption was that O'Neill had written a play reminiscent of his Connecticut childhood, but from what we have later learned, we now know that *Ah, Wilderness!* was a play not of literal "recollection" but of a kind of "might have been." It is true that Nat Miller has qualities of James O'Neill, Sr., that the elder son's behavior (or Uncle Sid's for that matter) suggests the dissipations of James, Jr., and that the young Richard is O'Neill himself. But *Ah, Wilderness!* is not a transcription of the youth which O'Neill experienced within the family; it is only that which, given a more benevolent Fate, he could have wished for. Fortunately, it is quite a good comedy, on a level well above the fluff of routine domestic farce. The serious undertones of strain within the Miller family, all plausible and all very human, serve to underline the constant proximity to disaster where so much of comedy exists. The drunkenness of Sid is hilarious; it is at the same time terribly pathetic. The rebellious Richard, a highly sensitive youth desperately seeking familial understanding, is the comic epitome of all "younger generations," but he is driven very close to disaster. The well-written "facts of life" scene suggests the familiar father-son embarrassments, but it departs from the "birds and bees" nonsense as Nat Miller warns his son how, when caught, to take care of himself properly. The O'Neill of waterfront bars and brothels is ever in the background.

The active producing career of Eugene O'Neill ceased in 1934 with the next to the last play to be staged in New York within his lifetime. It was an ignoble end, and after the promise of "rejoining the human race" demonstrated by *Ah, Wilderness!* the shock of *Days Without End* was doubly acute. In addition, it raised some of the most violent critical debates of any O'Neill play, all the more unfortunate because they were drawn along religious lines.

The story of John Worthing and his conversion, with the attendant "miracle" is, as a play, probably the worst thing O'Neill ever wrote, and that is, as we have seen, a strong statement. It creaks in every joint with dramatic devices of the most transparent sort. Its split personality of a protagonist demands one grotesquely masked actor and one in "mufti," who do little more than enter into a prolonged discussion of what is obviously O'Neill's own past, told in long, boring dialogues with a priest. The culmination is an embarrassingly bad scene of religious fervor. The discouraging aspect of the entire fiasco was the argument between lay critics, all of whom knew a bad play when they saw it and said so bluntly, and the religious commentators, Catholic and Protestant, who fervently insisted that laymen could

79

not identify a really good play on religion when it appeared right in front of them. The entire exchange of recriminations was a sad day for intelligent dramatic criticism.

The Nobel Prize came to Eugene O'Neill only two years after the fiasco of *Days Without End*, at a time when there was every reason to assume that his career would, for all that, continue to prosper. The prize did not seem so much a climactic reward as a recognition of heights achieved somewhere mid-point in a remarkably productive life. The promise of more and greater things was constantly in the air. Rumors told of the mighty cycle, *A Tale of Possessors Self-Dispossessed*, including anywhere from five to eleven plays and covering the history of an Irish-American family. The Theatre Guild announced from time to time that it would momentarily stage the "next" O'Neill play. But the years passed. Four, five, then ten, and twelve. A new generation of producers, actors, and audiences could scarcely recall who O'Neill was or the names of his important plays. Except for the flurry of publicity attending the prize, O'Neill was no longer news.

The O'Neill who arrived on the Pacific Coast in 1936, not to return to the East until a decade later, had become a figure as changed in many ways from the young revolutionary of the twenties as that earlier figure had been altered from the dissipated vagabond who had decided he would become an artist or nothing. One need only read the details of the nightmarish drinking bouts at one time shared with brother James as described by O'Neill's second wife, Agnes Boulton, to be aware that the teetotaller who retired to a Chinese-style country house in California was, in personal habit, a changed man. The O'Neill of Greenwich Village and Provincetown bohemianism had advanced to palatial manor houses in Bermuda, chateaux in France, and oceanside villas in Georgia, all complete with household retinues. The O'Neill that did not change, however, was the artist who refused to become a public celebrity, remaining aloof and secluded, always open to his few intimate friends, never to the prying reporter. The personal life of Eugene O'Neill and his family, although often filled with sensation, never became subject for gossiping columnists. When O'Neill asked to be let alone, there was no question that he meant it, and his wish was uniformly respected. Atop all his problems—the dissipations of son Shane, daughter Oona's marriage to Charlie Chaplin and subsequent disinheritance, and the tragic career and suicide of elder son Eugene, Jr.—was O'Neill's steadily deteriorating health, a nervous disorder akin to Parkinson's disease, that eventually incapacitated him for any creative work and resulted in the destruction of much of the nearly completed cycle. Ironically, even the award of the Nobel Prize itself could not be made under normal conditions, for O'Neill received it in a hospital bed in Oakland, California, where he was recovering from appendicitis.

Then, in 1946, came news that a new play was finally to be produced by the Theatre Guild. Amid great fanfare, including the first and only public press conference O'Neill ever held, and national magazine cover stories, *The Iceman Cometh* returned O'Neill to the New York stage he had at one time so strongly dominated. The public, alas, was not yet ready for the return of this voice from the past. *The Iceman*, O'Neill's play of New York's "lower depths" and the destructive pipe dreams by which mankind must live and die, could not hold the stage. No more plays appeared,

81

save *A Moon for the Misbegotten*, which could not survive the police censorship and casting difficulties of its road tryouts in 1950. O'Neill once more retired from view, this time to Marblehead, where further news of illnesses and domestic strife filtered out to a largely uninterested public. In 1953, Eugene O'Neill died, mourned only by his third wife and a handful of friends, virtually unnoted by the public that had once so strongly fought among themselves about his greatness.

The O'Neill revival that began in 1956 was unique because it did not represent so much a revival of interest in past works as an awareness of O'Neill as a writer of "new" plays; that is, a series of five never before available to the general public. First came *Long Day's Journey into Night* in Stockholm and New York, followed quickly by the sensational success of the off-Broadway revival of *The Iceman Cometh*. *A Moon for the Misbegotten* arose from the ashes for a respectable Broadway run, after which *A Touch of the Poet* from the *Self-Dispossessed* cycle brought general praise. Stockholm then produced in 1962 another of the cycle, *More Stately Mansions*, reconstructed from the original draft; publication of it by the Yale University Press followed in 1964. The one-act duologue, *Hughie*, closed out the series with a 1964 New York production. Volume upon volume of biography and criticism began to appear in the late 1950's, and university professors and students found O'Neill worthy of graduate-level teaching and research.

How do the later plays stand artistically beside the others? Very well, on the whole, but probably no more nor less successful than the good ones which preceded them. The gross Irish comedy and pathos of *A Moon for the Misbegotten*, with its giant virgin earth-mother, Josie, is effective, if heavy-handed. The ridiculous, strutting Cornelius Melody of *A Touch of the Poet* and his very humane wife are two of O'Neill's most sympathetic characterizations. *Hughie* is a colorful vignette of a failure. *More Stately Mansions*, still cumbersome despite severe pruning of the surviving manuscript, is a confusing drawn-out portrait of a poet turned robber baron, whose wife and mother, through his own devilish machinations, are pitted against each other in a deadly struggle for his soul. The battle is hardly worth it.

Among them all stands out the play that is probably O'Neill's over-all finest work. In the long evening's duration of *Long Day's Journey into Night*, O'Neill has created a piece of dramatic art very near the essence of classic tragedy. The Tyrone (O'Neill) family is plainly doomed. Its helpless, struggling members form a group protagonist driven into a desperate search to find themselves and to establish an acceptable relationship with each other. Seeking the aid of drink, drugs, money, and intellect, they drift farther apart, desperately wounding themselves and those they seek to love in an agony of wild, blind, slashing attacks. The love-hate forces that will destroy them simultaneously reveal the human dignity beneath; the theme of suffering, inchoate humanity and its terrifying need for understanding becomes universal. Although the play suffers in O'Neill's usual fashion of great length and ponderous repetitive dialogue, while the stage is drenched in whisky and curses to the point of supersaturation, its demonstration of O'Neill's awareness of the plight of ordinary men and women seeking so desperately to find meaning in their lives is the most skilled of his entire collection.

The critical minority who were unable to justify O'Neill's

choice as the Nobel Prize winner for literature in 1936 might not even now, some thirty years after, have changed their minds. But it would seem that, in the light of the body of work extant at the time, reinforced by subsequent productions, the choice was wise, appropriate, and inevitable. No writer in the contemporary theater has come close to the tragic vision that O'Neill so constantly, albeit unevenly, displayed. The American theater, furthermore, was visibly shaken by his impact and was made to look unto itself and, for the first time, to our permanent benefit, to take itself seriously.

Although he was often violently attacked for being vile, disgusting, and obscene, Eugene O'Neill was a man very much aware of human sensibilities. He may have sent his men and women into violent sexual clashes that he called human love, but they were not inhuman clashes. They were not a portrayal of the wild absurdities of life, nor were they filled with nihilistic despair. They are plays of deep concern for the fate that men have brought upon themselves not only because of their inability to find a meaningful God, but because of the lack of a meaningful relationship with each other. There is a constant hope, for O'Neill is in the true spirit of the tragic writer. Man may be trapped, and he may from time to time act with incomprehensible perversity, but he is still man, and his potential greatness is ever in the background. As O'Neill's protagonists strive and fail and strive again, they make the struggle worth the effort, and the inevitable doom that destroys them can never alter that fact.

PEARL BUCK

by Dody Weston Thompson

T HE NOBEL AWARDS to Sinclair Lewis in 1930 and Eugene
O'Neill in 1936 seemed to signal the European acceptance
of American letters at last. There should have been elation
when, two years later, the Nobel Prize for literature was
again offered to an American: this time to a woman, Pearl
S. Buck. But this woman, whose first novel had appeared a
scant eight years before, seemed an interloper. Moreover,
she had lived in China most of her life until 1934, and consequently all her stories were set there. It was true that five
of her eleven books had been international best sellers, and
her second novel, *The Good Earth*, upon its publication in
1931 had leaped from a springboard of critical hosannas to
a spectacular and sustained world-wide success that remains unparalleled to this day by any American author
except Mark Twain. But by 1938 her work was no longer
so acceptable to the literati, and the announcement of the
award raised a storm of protest. Was Theodore Dreiser's
durable career (and well-known desire for the coveted
honor) to go uncrowned after all? If the prize was to come

to an American woman, why not recognize long-established and deserving Willa Cather? Mass-circulation arbiters of taste like *Time* magazine would also have preferred Dreiser as an American choice, or Carl Sandburg or Van Wyck Brooks, while the more advanced savants proposed T. S. Eliot or Ernest Hemingway, both of whom had been publishing important works since the 1920's and before. Certainly for American college students of 1938 it was discussions of Eliot's "The Love Song of J. Alfred Prufrock" that kept them late awake in hotly argued dormitory sessions, not the best sellers of Pearl Buck, an author who for all her fame could hardly be seen on their literary horizons. The recipient was herself astonished at the unexpected news, and her first thought was widely reported to have been, *"O pu sin sing,"* a Chinese way of saying, "I don't believe it!"

That Pearl Buck's fiction should have been popular is entirely credible, given her exotic material, her considerable gift as a storyteller, her ability to show both sides of an issue with understanding, and the warmth (especially for her beloved Chinese people) that shone through her prose. *The Good Earth* is still memorable today, but the meteoric public response to it made publishing history. Launched on March 2, 1931, it went into a second printing before the end of the month and into a seventeenth before the end of the year. It sprang onto best-seller lists and stayed for two years; it was made into a Broadway play and a famous film; it won the Pulitzer Prize in 1932, the William Dean Howells Medal for Distinguished Fiction in 1935, and the culminating Nobel award in 1938. Its author, lionized and bemedaled, became an international celebrity. Translations were eventually authorized into more than thirty languages, spanning the globe from Sweden to Arabia, from France to India. There were known to be pirated editions in China, Japan, and at least three languages of the Soviet Union. Pearl Buck once wryly reported that in China she had seen "seven different translations, some in full and some in shortened versions. . . . Young writers lifted certain incidents and characters out of the book and wove amplified stories about them and sold them as original works." It has been authoritatively estimated that *The Good Earth* was at one point in the thirties known to just about the total reading public of the world. Statistics show that, by 1938, Pearl Buck had superseded the widely approved Eugene O'Neill in Sweden to become the most popular author there of any nationality.

Success to this degree is a phenomenon only intelligible in terms of a total context—personal, literary, and historical. Certainly it could not have been predictable. Publishers had repeatedly turned down her manuscripts because the public, they said, was not interested in books about China. Pearl Buck herself seemed an unlikely candidate for fame, quietly raising her family and teaching school half a world away, and finally in the late twenties, publishing a few modest articles and stories in American magazines. Her lifetime in China had imbued her with an ancient culture that was in those days still distant and mysterious to Westerners. She was brought to China as an infant by her American missionary parents, and except for college she did not return to the United States until 1934, when she was over forty. "I began in the Middle Ages," she herself has said. Her formative childhood years were spent in the flickering peace of the dying Manchu Dynasty. In 1900, when she was eight, the Boxer Rebellion, with its pig-tailed cadres convinced they were protected by unassailable magic from the bullets of the "foreign devils," signaled the start of the Middle Kingdom's long convulsive struggle toward the modern world. Hers was not the China of most foreigners (not even of most missionaries). By principle her parents lived among the Chinese population, and she was raised in the midst of teeming, inland Chinkiang, where the Yangtse River met the Grand Canal. She spoke Chinese before English and felt at home with Chinese friends. Many years later she wrote, "I grew up in a double world, the small clean Presbyterian world of my parents and the big, loving merry not-too-clean Chinese world," and titled her autobiography *My Several Worlds* in token of the duality of her inheritance.

If the Chinese ways of life that she absorbed were hoary with the cultural accretions of four thousand years, her birthright from her parents was also of a past and passing world, a powerful, mid-nineteenth-century and American pattern of thought—active, egalitarian, pioneering, upright, and compelled to service. Within the limits of that day and that profession, it was not a narrow heritage. Her scholarly father, a student of comparative religion who commanded four languages, made a lifetime project of translating the Bible from the original Greek into Chinese; from him she learned that Buddhism had an essential meeting ground with Christianity, a noble ethical tradition embodied in the Golden Rule. Her mother was from a cultivated family and had traveled in Europe when she was young; she could teach her children the language, literature, art, and music of the West. Yet her parents had been children during the American Civil War, and their view of life had long crystallized by the time they came to China in 1880. Their shining memories of America were passed intact, enshrined and polished like a fly in amber, to their children in a strange land. In this way, since she lacked the usual means of modifying the parental view by contemporary impressions outside the home, Pearl Buck's mold was irrevocably set a generation behind what would have been her normal one. If later she exchanged the ricksha for jet planes, if the deep peace of her childhood gave way to revolution, and she both read and traveled widely, her deepest roots nevertheless were locked away in time, as she herself had been in space. East versus West, Victorian versus twentieth-century values: her life and work turn on their interplay.

Under the circumstances it was not surprising that when her books began to appear in 1930, they reflected none of the literary and ideological ferment that had been seething in the West, whose literary prophets in England and America were voicing sterility and doom in the wake of the forces the twentieth century had loosed. James Joyce's *Ulysses* and T. S. Eliot's *The Waste Land* had both appeared in 1922, seminal works in the swelling tide of innovation and iconoclasm; the swing toward subjective presentation that had begun with Henry James was ending right inside the head of Molly Bloom. The realistic novels of social protest and satire from the United States by Sinclair Lewis, Dos Passos, Dreiser, Faulkner, Hemingway, and Fitzgerald represented another kind of response to the same overwhelming circumstance, the breakup of formerly sustaining values under the continued impact of Darwin, Freud, and Marx. Every Victorian political, moral, and aesthetic code was under fire.

Into such a literary milieu Pearl Buck introduced a series of Chinese peasant and family sagas of uncomplicated plot, constructed in conventional novel form, realistic and objective presentations told in simple, biblical-sounding language. The first appeared in the year that Sinclair Lewis received the Nobel award. *East Wind, West Wind* (which plainly showed its genesis from two short stories) was an unassuming volume whose dual and somewhat sentimental love story circled gently around the theme of the clash between generations, the conflict between the age-old Eastern ways and the new ideas invading China from the West. It was considered "promising"—and quickly went through three editions. In 1931 the outcome of the deepening worldwide depression, was uncertain. That year *The Good Earth* appeared, with the startling results we know, followed by its sequels, *Sons* in 1932 and *A House Divided* in 1935, which together comprised the trilogy called *The House of Earth*. *The Mother*, outside the trilogy, appeared meantime in 1934. In addition, Pearl Buck turned out with prolific ease during those years before the Nobel award *The Young Revolutionist*, a children's book, in 1933; perceptive biographies of her mother (*The Exile*) and her father (*Fighting Angel*) in 1936; her first novel with an American background, *This Proud Heart*, which was serialized in a ladies' magazine in 1938; and a massive, two-volume translation into English of a classic Chinese novel.

Why, when they were so far from the literary vanguard, was the response to these works so sweeping? Because they spoke to the poverty and uncertainty of the times. There hovered over them the certitudes of an inner-directed and Victorian spirit with a large and generous view of life, which could present values rather than seek them in a troubled world. In those Depression years *The Good Earth*'s vivid and compassionate picture of the bare subsistence level of the Chinese masses fed the fires of protest against social injustice, while at the same time offering the satisfactions of a rags-to-riches tale. The rise of Wang Lung and his wife O-lan, by dogged thrift and industry, from starvation in a drought year to a position of wealth and the establishment of a family dynasty is a success story par excellence in which the underdog wins against all the odds of man and nature—against the feudal social system on the one hand and on the other famine, flood, and drought. In the United States, "where every man can become President," this suited our notions of democracy and free will: did not a man's destiny lie in himself? The artists challenged that principle, but not as yet the general public.

There were other aspects of *The Good Earth* and *The Mother* that must have been especially appealing to those times. To an East wracked by social revolution, and a West whose moral and economic fabric increasingly gave way, the strong, dignified, and uncomplex narratives of the immemorial Chinese peasant life, told with a simplicity that could be translated readily and understood anywhere, stressed the eternal verities of soil and season, of the fruit of the earth and the womb, the quintessential human facts of birth, love, laughter, sorrow, death. *The Good Earth*—how meaningful a title to all those dispossessed by want in cities. How comforting, in the midst of devastating material and spiritual flux, to glimpse stability, to be so convincingly reminded of life's perpetual self-renewal, the ever returning spring after winter in the changeless cycle of the earth's turning. It was the expression of a peculiarly Eastern view, its symbol the cycle, the circle, its source in conceptions of karma and reincarnation. Certainly the cyclic form appears over and over in Pearl Buck's novels of the thirties. Within the grand cycle in the trilogy of the rise and fall of Wang Lung's *House of Earth*, there are smaller ones. Wang Lung comes from the land, and in the end returns to it from the courts of his rich city home, while his sons plot over his dying head to sell the good earth he had so painfully acquired to found the fortunes of his house. Just so the wheel of life comes full around in the last pages of *The Mother*. The old Chinese mother's grief as she reviews the sum of her life's loss and sorrows is briefly transfigured into joy upon the birth of a new child, her grandson. "Pearl Buck's true theme," wrote Phyllis Bentley in 1935, "is the continuity of life."

The mother is intended as a timeless embodiment in a Chinese setting: she and all the cast remain nameless throughout. But behind the universal implications, and behind the veil of Chinese life, can be discerned moving throughout the book the essential figure in the dance, venerable earth-mother herself, the fertile goddess celebrating an ancient and feminine mystique:

> ... this woman was such a one as could live well content with the man and the children and think of nothing else at all. To her—to know the fullness of the man's frequent passion, to conceive by him and know life growing within her own body, to feel this new flesh take shape and grow, to give birth and feel a child's lips drink at her breast—these were enough. To rise at dawn and feed her house and tend the beast, to sow the land and reap its fruit, to draw water at the well for drink, to spend days upon the hills reaping the wild grass and know the sun and wind upon her, these were enough. . . .

Such a state of being was for obvious reasons more empathetic to women than to men. Miss Bentley in the *English*

Journal called the book "that miniature masterpiece," and
Florence Ayscough in *The Saturday Review of Literature*
called Pearl Buck "a novelist to whom life unfolds its
secret." To this, however, Geoffrey Stone in *Commonweal*
demurred irately, "What the whole book embodies is not
the universally significant but an indiscriminate celebration
of the warm and fluctuant animal substructure of life—
which, whatever might be the moralist's reasons, the book
reviewer must condemn as boring." David Garnett in *The
New Statesman and Nation* concurred, calling it "a crude
wooden story told in a false affected style."

If there was any public and critical consensus before her
Nobel award (she was ignored by some of the highbrow
critics from first to last), it was typified by the words of
J. Donald Adams of the *New York Times*, who wrote, "She
has rendered the life of a people deeply alien from ourselves
in terms of universal human values." Dr. Per Hallstrom of
the Swedish Academy, in his address at the Concert Hall
in Stockholm preceding the presentation of the Nobel
award, noted that Pearl Buck "had found her mission as
interpreter to the Occident of the nature and being of
China," and indeed it seemed to most of her readers that
she had opened at last the long-closed door of understanding between East and West, a door shut since the days of
Kipling's assertion that never the twain should meet. She
had humanized that mythical and faceless figure, the In-
scrutable Oriental, who emerged now from her pen as
Universal Man. Wang Lung manifested the same needs,
joys, and sorrows as people everywhere; he was not so much
an individual as he was everyman.

The modern reader, in fact, is struck by a curious paradox
in this regard: it is exactly how un-foreign these novels

seem. Moving in a vivid world of Chinese custom, in a spiritual landscape seen always understandingly through Chinese eyes, Pearl Buck's major characters of that period were, nevertheless, so "universal," so recognizable anywhere, as to seem only incidentally "Chinese." One gets no real sense in these novels of an ethos that was in actuality profoundly different from the West. Nowhere, for example, is it shown what constitutes a Taoist, Buddhist or Confucian, their distinctions and similarities, or their considerable distances from European thought (although some pervasive aspects of their philosophies affected her writing). Pearl Buck was not interested in stressing differences. Out of intense conviction she aimed, unconsciously in these first books perhaps, to demonstrate similarity in order to promote understanding, to allow the West to cross the gap—or rather to show there was no human gap at all, only a factitious cultural one. "In essentials," she was quoted as saying in the *China Weekly Review*, "the Chinese are the same as Europeans. And yet when I am asked what they are like I do not know. They are not like this and that, they are people."

It is not surprising, therefore, that when she decided to translate into English one of the three most famous Chinese novels, a popular classic for centuries, her choice should have rested on that one which was a majestic pageant of the people, "a great procession of humanity," as she called it in her introduction. Since its title *Shui-hu chuan* (or "Water-margins novel"), allusive enough in Chinese, was meaningless in English, she significantly retitled it *All Men Are Brothers*.

With her attitude and works of such libertarian bent and humanistic merit, so much in accord with Nobel's injunc-

tion that his prize go to "the best works of an idealistic
nature," it seems understandable that the Nobel award in
1938 went to Pearl Buck for "rich and epic genuine por-
trayals of Chinese peasant life, and for masterpieces of
biography." It is likely that she touched special chords of
Swedish feeling as well. Sweden had shown a persistent
interest in family and peasant epics, especially those distant
in time or place, as evidenced by previous Nobel awards,
such as the one to Knut Hamsun and also, interestingly, to
all three of the previous women winners, Selma Lagerlöf,
the Sardinian writer Grazia Deledda, and Sigrid Undset.
Just the previous year the Academy had bestowed laurels
on Roger Martin du Gard, the French author of a great
roman-fleuve.

There also emanated lightly from Pearl Buck's work a
whiff of Ibsen's *A Doll's House* theme, which may have had
special interest for Scandinavians. She dealt with it cen-
trally in *This Proud Heart*, her final novel before receiving
the Nobel Prize. Full of clichés, the book unfortunately
descended perilously near to pot-boiling, its only salvation
being the thoughtful nature of its subject, which examined
the heroine's conflict between her powerful feminine drives
—home-making, man-loving, and child-bearing—and the
more objective goals demanded by the artist in her, which
required that as a sculptress she find an essential and independent self-fulfillment. The source of whatever feminist
conflict resided in Pearl Buck herself is revealed in the two
biographies of her parents. Despite their remarkable objectivity, they make clear her greater attachment to her
warm-hearted, beauty-loving, and spirited mother (always
passionately torn between God and humanity, who lost four
of seven children before refusing to follow her husband's

95

missionary wandering through cholera-infested China) than to her more austere "fighting angel" of a father, who believed in the Pauline doctrine that "the man was head of the woman" and was too busy saving souls "with that sword-like singleness of heart" to see the living needs of whatever human beings were before him. Pearl Buck called it "a magnificent imperialism of the spirit." "For he was a spirit," she wrote, "and a spirit made by that blind certainty, that pure intolerance, that zeal for mission, that contempt for man and earth, that high confidence in heaven, which our forefathers bequeathed to us." The biographies were powerful considerations in swinging the award that year, and Selma Lagerlöf personally told Pearl Buck that they were the decisive factor in her own favorable vote.

Of greater significance in explaining the Swedish response, however, was Pearl Buck's transmutation of her religious heritage into a lively egalitarianism that might be said to parallel the Swedish translation of its historically intense religiosity into the most advanced social legislation of the Western democracies. Each was putting the Christian ethic into action. If O'Neill sought God, Pearl Buck accepted Him and went on to do good works. Neutralist Sweden responded heartily to this apolitical, supra-national idealist, whose dual cultural tradition and subsequent world-wide travel had given her an objectivity of vision beyond the usual national myopias, who had widely proclaimed in print her antitotalitarian principles and publicly refused an invitation to stop in Hitler's Germany en route to the award ceremonies. The Swedish newspapers began calling her "The Pearl," and her Swedish visit became a personal triumph.

In the Concert Hall at Stockholm, on the traditional date

of December 10, Per Hallström spoke of the "profound and warm humanity" of her general outlook and stated that in its choice the Academy felt it had acted "in harmony and accord with the aim of Alfred Nobel's dreams for the future." As his words implied, it was incumbent on the jurors to be swayed by such considerations, since it was manifestly Nobel's intention, in the literary field as in the others, to single out works that would benefit mankind. From the beginning this has constituted a central dilemma of the committee's deliberations—the unhappy pendulum on which its decisions yearly swing—whether to honor primarily an achievement in ethics or aesthetics. By the broadest definition it can be said that any masterpiece should benefit mankind; but as humanitarianism is usually much easier to recognize than genius, whose manifestations are apt to be thorny and ahead of time, the committee, being human and often conservative, has tended to honor obvious morality before high art. Viewed in this light, it is not surprising that the award to Pearl Buck antedated by so many years those to Eliot, Hemingway, and Faulkner, all of whom were publishing before she was, but who had to wait either to be softened by time, as in the case of Hemingway, or to be certified as artists by international critical acclaim. The award to John Steinbeck seems to represent one of those backward swings of the pendulum: the parallels between *The Good Earth* and *The Grapes of Wrath* are obvious.

No doubt the committee members felt that in Pearl Buck they had found a happy combination of art and idealism; and they were, after all, only following the dictum laid down for them; but the literary world, whose initial enthusiasm for *The Good Earth* had cooled under the uneven quality of the following works, was under no such constraint. The critics insisted on an assessment by standards of literary excellence alone and continued to grumble at the choice. They were thinking, of course, in terms of the twentieth century, in terms of Joyce, Eliot, and Kafka, while Pearl Buck's style and spirit alike stayed firmly planted in other times and other worlds, whose influences acted to confound the aesthetics by which the West was judging her. When she took up writing as a profession (she had been writing actively since childhood), she naturally employed for fiction what was essentially the classic Western novel form, gleaned from the high Victorians on her parents' bookshelves, and particularly from Dickens, whom she read once through every year for nine years in her youth. "If before twenty I read Dickens, after twenty I read Dreiser and after him, Sinclair Lewis," she said in *My Several Worlds*. Thus her manner was realism, strung out along the straightforward chronology of a presumed objective time. Her work contained neither experiment with form nor investigation of the psyche: one could read it, safely unaware that it had been written in the era ushered in by Freud. Her leading characters were everyman—and everywoman—whose various characteristics, displayed serially in time, represented not so much the inevitable responses of a unique individual as typical and generalized human reactions in a given situation. Her minor characters were what the West had once called "humours," physical and temperamental types with the flatness natural to such creations.

The West, meantime, had been busily exchanging this horizontal novel form for a more vertical and static one of depth exploration, in which the only actuality, as in *The*

Trial, was apt to be subjective, and the surface action so subordinated that vast novels, like *Ulysses*, could take place within the confines of one day even while encompassing a life (indeed, a world), or the action of whole books, like William Golding's later *Pincher Martin*, consist of a man's fantasy in the moment before he drowns. The West expected now not two dimensions from a character but four at least—not Wang Lung Everypeasant but Mrs. Dalloway. If the critics approved a woman writer, it was a woman like Virginia Woolf.

But delineation in depth of a rounded, crotchety, and specific human being was not Pearl Buck's mode. She was working in an idiom older even than the objective realism of the nineteenth-century West, one which had come to her by way of the folk tradition of the indigenous Chinese novel, where, as in all folk-telling, from Icelandic sagas to Homeric tales, from the *Morte d'Arthur* to the *Shui-hu*, character is given, not explained. While young, she had absorbed this literature and had just spent four years immersed in the translation of one of its great examples during the very same period that she was writing her early novels. She was aware of its influence, and when asked to speak on a literary subject for the Nobel award, she chose to give a lecture that was later published under the title "The Chinese Novel."

To understand the Chinese novel, it is necessary first to know that historically there existed in China not one but three literatures, the only official one being the literature of the upper-class scholar-bureaucrats, who presided over it unchallenged as the only literate elements in the society. In this scholarly tradition, very much bound up with the pervasive Confucian doctrines, it was held that true literature must have social utility (such as the moral value or philosophical content of history, criticism, or religious commentary) and must be written in Wen-li, the classical language. Its works were often highly allusive, and the use of what we would call cliché phrases was considered meritorious. (*East Wind, West Wind* had to be corrected for clichés before publication, as Pearl Buck had in the Chinese way larded the manuscript with them.)

At the other end of the social scale a rich and ancient oral literature flourished, a professional art capable of rising to unexpected heights of complexity and skill. It existed in China right down into the present century. In 1959 there were still thirty-three known storytellers in Yangchow alone, one of whom had as his specialty the saga of Wu-sang, a hero of the *Shui-hu*, which took him seventy-five two-hour sessions to narrate when recorded and included almost a million characters.

Between the two stood the vernacular literature, written not in Wen-li but in the everyday speech of the illiterate so that they could understand it when it was read aloud. Until the twentieth century, it was considered merely an amusement for the common man. Although read by the literate as well, who could not resist the pleasures of fiction, it had no acceptance as a serious literary form. Over the centuries great story cycles formed and re-formed around particular characters or subjects, like that of the robber band in the *Shui-hu*. The Chinese novelist was free to cut or add at will, to rewrite and rearrange earlier versions. He functioned, in fact, much like those modern Chinese who "pirated" and rewrote versions of *The Good Earth*, and who were after all following a long-sanctioned Chinese custom.

The foremost attribute of this Chinese folk tradition was,

as might be expected, fast-moving action coupled with simplicity of style and vocabulary. As Pearl Buck explained in her Nobel address, "the story tellers . . . found that the style [the people] loved best was one which flowed along, clearly and simply, in the short words which they themselves used every day, with no other technique than occasional bits of description, only enough to give vividness to a place or a person, and never enough to delay the story. Nothing must delay the story." (Here was a source of the simplicity of her own Chinese novels, and the often laconic aptness of her descriptions, a source equal to the influence of the King James Version of the Bible, which during her childhood had been daily read aloud.) She went on to explain that by action she did not mean crude action alone: it must spring from character. To the Chinese, vividness of character was so important that "*Shui Hu Chuan* was considered one of their three greatest novels, not primarily because it is full of the flash and fire of action, but because it portrays so distinctly one hundred and eight characters that each is to be seen separate from the others." Furthermore, the portrayal of character had to be "by the character's own action and words rather than by the author's explanation." What an amount of European work would be excluded by such a condition, almost the whole of the modern novel and certainly all of Henry James.

This distaste for the author's imposition between the story and the reader relates to a Chinese concept of the novel and the novelist that is particularly foreign to the West. Pearl Buck noted that "a good novelist . . . should be 'tse ran,' that is, natural, unaffected, and so flexible and variable as to be wholly at the command of the material that flows through him. . . . We should never be able, merely by reading pages, to know who wrote them." How opposite to our cult of the development of style is this notion of a self-effacing author, who, like a clear vessel, must transmit but not color with his personality the life that "flows through him." If these standards were applied to Western literature, Shakespeare might retain his stature but Proust would shrink to insignificance. We here come upon literary differences no longer explainable on grounds of the folk origins of the Chinese novel, for we are touching on ideas deeply imbedded in Chinese thought. This unassuming quality of the author relates to the modesty so stressed in Confucianism; at a deeper level it reflects the much smaller emphasis given to development of the ego in traditional Chinese culture, where the individual was of subordinate importance to the family. In a similar way, it seems that the frequent and accepted use in Chinese fiction of the anecdotal, the apparently fortuitous happening, coincidence, or any unexpected turn of the story, has to do with an age-old preoccupation of the Chinese mind with the chance aspect of events, as opposed to the emphasis the West places on causality. The capricious in Western literature is relegated largely to the realms of fantasy; in realism it is usually not welcome; the author, we say, did not "prepare" us, by which we usually mean he did not show the causes building up so that we could then accept the event as a logical effect.

All these influences bear directly on Pearl Buck's work. We note the strict authorial distance kept in most of her early Chinese novels. One comment about *The Good Earth* was that its manner was so objective that one could not tell from internal evidence whether it had been written by a woman or a man. Any tendency to moralize was held at bay by the code of the Chinese novelist. A common critical complaint has been against Mrs. Buck's liberal use of accident and the *deus ex machina* to move her plot along. And above all, of course, the importance of plot in her work—or as she called it, story, always story.

To explain, however, is never to explain away. We may illuminate the forces in her working against a unified approach, but it is the question of that final lack that is important. For the trouble was not that Pearl Buck used an out-dated Western novel form, modified by Chinese influences (or the other way about), but that she never mastered either form in its purity, nor succeeded in her efforts at a synthesis. She came closest in her pre-Nobel novels, and of these *The Good Earth* remains by far the best, in its proportions and in its unity of style and content. Both *The Good Earth* and *The Mother* have an emotional coherence lent by the passionate respect and admiration for the Chinese peasant that came pouring out when she sat down to write of them. (She wrote *The Mother* immediately following *The Good Earth*, although they were published three years apart.) Both Malcolm Cowley and Henry Seidel Canby, in re-evaluations after the Nobel award, gave credit to *The Good Earth* as a "masterpiece," although they hedged their definition. Paul A. Doyle aptly put it in his recent re-examination of Pearl Buck that in *The Good Earth* "realism and romanticism blend in just the right proportions. Life is given the glow of legend, and legend is given the aura of life."

But in the sequels to *The Good Earth* her technical deficiencies dominate. *Sons* has all the ingredients of a major tragic figure in the character of Wang Lung's son who becomes a small-time Chinese war lord. Wang the Tiger is a man who sets out to snatch power and money in this time-honored Chinese way, only to find he has not the requisite ruthlessness: he is flawed by compassion, yet trapped in his self-created and now empty role. He is unable to establish a right relationship with a woman (he chooses impossible ones) and compensates by an obsessive and self-defeating love for his son, which eventually betrays him into neglecting what petty empire he has achieved. It falls into dissolution about him as he grows into an unfulfilled old age. What an unforgettable portrait this might have been—a character both unique and distinctly Chinese. But it is never realized, and has not even the clarity and vigor of this accurate description. The extreme authorial impersonality comes closer in this book to comedy, which requires that distance, than to tragedy, in which emotional participation is a requisite; and part way through the author wanders off, in the loose way permissible in the more formless Chinese novel, in pursuit of the story of Wang the Tiger's son, leaving the father to fade into the background. *A House Divided* pursues Wang the Tiger's son through increasingly complex modern urban environments (including the United States and Shanghai), following the unfolding of his mind as it comes to grips with China's revolution and the modern world in general. But the simplified style of the peasant epics, though still employed, is no longer fitting; the "show, not tell" dictate of the Chinese novelists is left behind, yet without the benefits that modern Western techniques would have conferred in the exploration of inner growth; and the formless sprawl of this novel, while perhaps true to life, needed the shaping of an artist's control to carry the *conviction* of truth that is the only essential for the reader.

From the first, Pearl Buck equated the formal disciplines

of art, as it was understood by novelists in the West, with the stifling formalism of the Chinese intellectuals who had for centuries dessicated the vigor of the classic Chinese literature. At the same time, her scholarly Confucian tutor had instilled the intellectuals' notion that a reputable writer did not condescend to the production of novels, and this discouragement in her youth, coupled with her family's mild disapproval on religious grounds, had the result of more or less permanently lowering the novel in her estimation, despite her master's degree in English literature earned at Cornell in 1926. Sinclair Lewis took her to task for this attitude when they were guests once at a literary dinner at which she spoke. She modestly told the guests "that a mere teller of tales is not to be considered a literary figure, and that my novels were only stories to amuse people." Sinclair Lewis objected, "You must not minimize yourself, neither must you minimize your profession. A novelist has a noble function." Many years later she stated in a lecture at the Columbia School of Journalism, "I do not consider either the writing or reading of novels one of the necessities of life. Millions of people in China, at least, exist intelligently and happily without reading novels." Hers was a nature for whom life would always be more important than literature, and the value of people always the highest value in life. In the peroration of her Nobel address she made a clear and crucial statement of her position:

> The people of China forged their own literature apart from letters. And today this is what lives . . . and all the formal literature, which was called art, is dead. . . . Like the Chinese novelists, I have been taught to want to write for these people. If they are reading their magazines by the million, then I want my stories there. . . . No, a novelist must not think of

pure literature as his goal . . . . He is a story teller in a village tent and by his stories he entices people into his tent. He need not raise his voice when a scholar passes. But he must beat all his drums when a band of poor pilgrims pass . . . . To them he must cry, "I, too, tell of gods!"

Between the lines one senses a defensive reaction to the "stone-throwing" of the critics, and it is difficult not to conclude that this played a part in deflecting her from strictly aesthetic goals. From that period her development was more as a moralist and philanthropist than as a dedicated writer. Her activities ranged from the founding of the East and West Association for the promotion of mutual understanding to the writing of radio plays for the FBI during wartime. In a remarkable easy and lucid prose style she discussed everything from the war between men and women to actual war, from orphans to atom bombs. Her prodigious, restless energy spilled over into countless projects, and in a stream of books, pamphlets, articles, and lectures she commented on major internal and international issues. Racial equality became a major theme, as did freedom everywhere. Like her contemporary, Wendell Willkie, she envisioned one world, living in an accord based on the Golden Rule.

She seemed gradually to cease caring about development of the novel as an expressive art form and to pursue more and more its uses as propaganda, making less and less distinction between her aesthetic and her "missionary" aims. Many of her later novels became largely vehicles for her humanitarian themes. She was her father's daughter; there was something of the sermon or the tract about them: story was the mere sugar-coating to make the medicine go down.

Her talent for story assured her a large audience, and her influence for good has not been negligible, particularly in loosening the bonds of racial intolerance in the United States among her women readers. Today she stands, not as an artist, but in her chosen role of teller of tales—morality tales—to the people.

The impetus for these worthy preoccupations seems to rise from more profound levels of her being than simply her clerical family background corroborated by the benevolent aspects of the Buddhist and Confucian ethic. For all its active, worldly accomplishment and concern with intellectual themes—traditionally masculine prerogatives—hers has been an essentially feminine career. The signs can be traced through the repeated celebration of motherhood and the life-force in her novels to a lifelong concern for children expressed by the adoption of children herself, the founding of orphanages, and writing stories for children. In her most recent book she states, "I charm children." It could equally be said that children hypnotize her. Her ingrained sense of responsibility seems to stem from this instinctive motherhood. It is as though her original love for children expanded to include mankind. Her deep concern for the world's people has much the air about it of a mother's concern for the members of her brood: They may be wayward, sometimes unruly, but they are to be forgiven, guided, and, above all, loved. Even each of her charming books for children has a moral. She is the moral mother of us all. She fits, indeed, into that great American feminine tradition, Victorian in spirit, New England in conscience—though in her case a conscience purged of Puritanism by the robust Chinese life so long observed—whose line comes down through Harriet Beecher Stowe and Louisa May

Alcott to Eleanor Roosevelt: the ranks of American women who have given service with the pen.

There seems to be no real quarrel with the low critical estimation of the main body of her work. Pearl Buck wrote in careless haste (her books now total over seventy) with predictable results. A good tale well told has always been a solace and a satisfaction to mankind. But even when the dross settles from her prodigious and uneven output, it will be difficult to redress the balance of her later books, which display at one time or another, and sometimes all at once, careless lack of control of point of view, cliché characters, a sentimental Pollyannaism, a scarcely veiled didacticism, and a lack of depth despite a breadth of theme. It is only necessary to compare *The Patriot*, which was published in 1939, with André Malraux's classic published six years earlier, *La Condition Humaine*, known in English as *Man's Fate*. Each takes place during exactly the same period of Chinese history and even involves the same historical incident, the great Shanghai uprising of 1927. *La Condition Humaine*, though flawed, is a flawed work of art; *The Patriot* pales beside its utterly convincing and passionate complexity. As Edmund Wilson said when talking about Hemingway in a related context, Malraux is "not a moralist staging a melodrama, but an artist exhibiting situations the values of which are not simple."

Pearl Buck's fiction is indeed too simple for adults in our effete and complex age. For when the means are crude, illusion, on which all realistic art depends, collapses. Such work is then convincing only to the young, which is to say the unsophisticated of any age, who are credulous, and, like all primitive beings, more open to illusion than the worldly. Only a Candide can believe Pangloss, and events teach him not to. Now that her work is no longer a revelation of the Orient (though this quality gives it some lasting historical value), it is read not so much by all the people as by the young. It is revealing that when asked on television in 1965 to name his favorite authors, a young Korean student unhesitatingly replied, "Tolstoi and Pearl Buck." In this country, too, it is the student who regularly takes her books from library shelves; everywhere it is the idealist, one whose youthful hopefulness has not been eroded by experience. He can share her essential optimism, her belief that human nature is basically good and the world perfectible by rational means. It is another of her nineteenth-century aspects; it is not the view of an Eliot, a Camus, a Sartre, or a Beckett.

Nowadays we tend to dismiss all "good works" or discussion of them, since Freud made all altruistic motivation suspect. At best, we have transmuted them to the existentialist theory of commitment, based on personal psychological needs rather than objective ideals. Nevertheless, a contemporary evaluation depends on whether Pearl Buck is to be judged as artist or humanitarian, and as always that decision turns on the bias of the commentator. Thus Kenneth Tynan, reviewing in 1959 her play *A Desert Incident,* which debated the degree to which scientists are morally responsible for the use to which their knowledge is put, first tore the piece to shreds on aesthetic grounds, but then supported the author because of her thesis and conclusions. "I realize that considerations like these are not supposed to affect the judgment of a theater critic," Mr. Tynan concluded, "yet she chose the most important subject in the world, and though she handled it vaguely and emotionally, she came down on the side of life. . . . Because of her choice and her commitment, I am prepared to forgive Miss Buck a good deal."

T. S. ELIOT

by James V. Baker

WHEN T. S. ELIOT received the Nobel Prize for literature in 1948, he was the fourth American and the first American poet to be so honored. There is no doubt that he deserved the award. Yet the choice of Eliot marked a departure from the type of writers who had usually been recipients of the prize. Eliot's work was more esoteric and less in contact with the popular mind.

He won the Nobel Prize just a decade after Pearl Buck. This dramatic conjunction of names raises critical questions concerning the criteria of the judges in awarding the prize; nevertheless, in the house of literature there are many mansions, and, in the nature of things, Eliot's work, though profound, is more caviar to the general public than that of many previous winners. The prize was given him for his ability to cut into the consciousness of his generation and "for his outstanding, pioneer contribution to present-day poetry." Johannes Edfelt, Swedish translator and writer, said that his works have brought about a revolution in the poetic means of expression. Anders Österling, permanent secretary of the Swedish Academy and chairman of the Nobel Prize Committee, remembers that the discussions were not at all controversial and that the literary members of the Swedish Academy—the poets and writers—were eager supporters of his candidacy.

Eliot's poetry may be divided into two principal periods: the first, his secular, skeptical phase, when a reason for being is sought, culminating in *The Waste Land* (1922) and "The Hollow Men" (1925); the second, his Christian phase, during which he wrote *Ash-Wednesday* (1930), *Four Quartets* (1943), and the whole series of his verse plays. We shall now examine his poems and plays to see what qualities they exhibit which justify the distinguished award of the Nobel Prize.

The early poems give the impression of cleverness, wit, and sophistication, but they also strongly convey a feeling of nausea and disgust. They give the impression of having been inspired by a sensitivity that is disaffected towards and nauseated by modern commercialized society. The poems are, in fact, a mask, and what is hidden behind their front is the intense personal suffering of the author. The Eliot type of sensibility is one that above all demands order and meaning. Not finding it, the keen searchlight of the author's perception picks on now this detail, now that, yet everywhere a sense of nothingness pervades the scene:

> *The worlds revolve like ancient women*
> *Gathering fuel in vacant lots.*
>
> ("Preludes, IV")

Eliot's first book of poems, *Prufrock and Other Observations* (1917), and his second, *Poems* (1920), will be considered together as representative of his early phase. The longer poems in these two volumes, "The Love Song of J. Alfred Prufrock," "Portrait of a Lady," and "Gerontion" are interior monologues; we are inside someone's consciousness and that consciousness is usually male. One cannot exactly speak of these poems as dramatic monologues in the manner of Browning, for in Browning the person spoken to seems to be objectively present; in "Prufrock" the monologue is of Prufrock with himself, and we are eavesdroppers deep within the inner citadel of his awareness. At the opening of the poem Prufrock is aware of externals, the sunset, the city streets; later in the poem the level of consciousness deepens until the innermost and deepest level of the psyche is reached. Class consciousness is present also. Prufrock is aware of tedious streets and one-night cheap hotels and of lonely men in shirt sleeves, leaning out of windows; he is conscious that other men are lonely, too, and of the vast, teeming life of the slums; he is conscious of it, but not participant in this sleazy but vital life. He is locked within himself and his own feelings. Patently, as the poem's epigraph intimates, he is in hell, one of the many purgatories and hells that abound in Eliot's work from beginning to end. Prufrock's "I have measured out my life with coffee spoons" should be linked with "His laughter tinkled among the teacups" in "Mr. Apollinax." The difference is that Mr. Apollinax (said to be suggested by Bertrand Russell) is alarmingly vital, while Prufrock among the coffee cups is dying of alarm. He feels a pin through his thorax and his wings extended in an entomologist's showcase when he is under the gaze of critical women: An object under another's gaze, as Sartre would have it. A cultured person, he is more sensitive than Shelley's sensitive plant, for he curls up within himself in a tight-fisted ball at the very thought of his nerve patterns being exposed on a magnified cinerama screen.

There is more living phenomenology in the images of the few lines in "Prufrock" than may be encountered in pages and pages of abstract phenomenological philosophy. We are at the center of the consciousness of a timid man, and the way his consciousness is inserted into his world, where, so to speak, his psychological shoe pinches, is instantly present to our consciousness, too. His consciousness intends the image of the crab and our consciousness intends it simultaneously. "Prufrock," then, is an essay in practical phenomenology, an exposure of suffering. The root of that suffering is that nothing founds Prufrock's being. He has not had, in Tillich's words, the courage to be; neither has he had the courage to choose—which amounts really to the same thing. The fact that Prufrock's life is meaningless reduces it to misery. No religion, no love, no vital center, no outgoing, no giving of himself to others confers upon it virility or dignity. As Prufrock submerges into the chambers of the sea, where in a sexual fantasy he is wreathed by mermaids, we submerge, too, into his submarine and greenly silent world, his ultimate womb, where the wish for death lies deepest of all; when he surfaces and hears the sound of human voices (everyday reality breaking in), we become terribly aware of what it is to be lost. "Portrait of a Lady," the companion piece in the 1917 volume, is perhaps a little less masterfully brought off than "Prufrock," but it is hardly less to be prized for its psychological insight.

"Gerontion" has the initial position in the 1920 volume. The mask is that of an old man, and once again the poem is an interior monologue. He meditates on his own history frankly and intimately. We find even this early in Eliot the high valuation of action, commitment, and involvement; war itself is not the worst of evils. "I was neither at the hot gates / Nor fought in the warm rain." Gerontion feels the corruption of inaction as he stiffens in a rented house. The same valuation is expressed later in *The Waste Land* in the lines that express the thought that it is bad to have missed "The awful daring of a moment's surrender / Which an age of prudence can never retract." Gerontion's feeling of dryness, of a dry rot eating away his spirit, his desperate need of the bold and vital, are powerfully expressed in these words: "In the juvescence of the year / Came Christ the tiger." This image is of special interest because it states a theme found throughout Eliot's poems. Christ is associated with the sacrifices of the fertility rituals (the Dionysiac ritual was in the spring). What leaps out at us is the "tigerlike vitality of Christ," a terrifying vitality like that of Blake's "Tyger." But the "Gerontion" poem not only has Gerontion's meditation upon his personal history; it has a meditation upon the larger subject of human history, beginning, "History has many cunning passages, contrived corridors." This passage and the one following about "chilled delirium" and "the wilderness of mirrors," with their Jacobean flavor, are among the most effective rhetorically that Eliot has written. The saturated mind of Gerontion contains all of human history in solution.

The Waste Land (1922) is probably the most famous and controversial poem of the twentieth century. Although Eliot and the common man have uncommonly little in common except feelings and bodies, and although the poem is too recondite in its range of learning to be taken warmly to the popular breast, Eliot has succeeded in communicating a feeling about our civilization, and something of his attitude has seeped through to the popular mind and become part of contemporary consciousness in general. People were only dimly aware of how they felt about their experience in London after World War I; Eliot had the genius to tell them how they felt about it, to articulate their unexpressed feelings for them. One criterion of what is good in literature is this: anything is good that explains people to themselves. Eliot put his finger upon the living pulse of the age and expressed what it is like to be conscious in the twentieth century. His concern, it is now clear, was not with himself and his personal sufferings; it was with the fate of Western civilization as a whole.

It is at this time rather hard to recapture the first surreptitious enthusiasm of reading *The Waste Land* near to the time when it first appeared. One's elders disapproved of it or had not heard of it, and it had all the pleasure of the forbidden or the contraband. Since then it has become assigned reading to sophomores in survey courses in college, and it has had one indubitable effect: thousands of persons who might not otherwise have heard of Jessie Weston or Sir James Frazer have taken the prescribed course in *From Ritual to Romance* and *The Golden Bough*. Indeed, this has become part of the ritual of literature in our universities.

Joyce's *Ulysses* and Eliot's *The Waste Land* both appeared in the same year (1922). Eliot praised Joyce for using the Homeric myth of Odysseus as a means of imposing some order upon the immense panorama of futility that is modern history. Eliot likewise used myth for a similar purpose. "The whole structure of Eliot's poems," as Stephen Spender has said in *The Destructive Element*, "is based on

116

certain primitive rituals and myths." To organize a poem on such a basis at the time Eliot did it was an original departure. To use the wasteland of Grail legend as the basic metaphor of the poem and as equivalent to spiritual sterility was, in fact, a positive stroke of genius.

Fundamental to an understanding of the poem is a realization of what Eliot meant by "Unreal City," the phrase prominently used in Part I, "The Burial of the Dead," and repeated elsewhere in the poem. The expression "Unreal City" seems foreign to ordinary common sense; what is more real than London? The travel agency in New York which will book one's passage by sea or by air assumes that it is real, and when one arrives at one's destination, the tide of traffic at Piccadilly or up and down Oxford Street is real enough. Preposterous, then, to speak of the city as unreal! At this point we are brought up against the all-important distinction between appearance and reality which runs throughout Eliot's work. Eliot's standards are never naturalistic or realistic ones; to him the temporal is merely the ephemeral or the illusory. The "timekept city" where the values are commercial ones is altogether unreal.

The Waste Land has a dramatic character and would lend itself to radio production as a play for announcer and several voices. There is the immediacy, for instance, of "Marie, hold on tight" in the bobsled incident, a moment of genuine life in the memory of a person who has grown up to bored sophistication. The dramatic quality is particularly strong in Part II, called "The Game of Chess." The testimony of Robert Speaight, who has played one thousand times the role of Becket in *Murder in the Cathedral*, is interesting on this point. Speaking of *The Waste Land*, he says:

This I still regard as the summit of Eliot's poetry and far more dramatic—I am almost tempted to say—far more theatrical—than anything that he has written for the stage. Here then was an opportunity for impersonation—Madame Sosostris, the voices in the pub, the bank clerk, the couple in the canoe—richer than anything in the plays. The rhythms of the poem had a variety which I have discovered nowhere except in Shakespeare.

Indeed, one could make a strong case and argue that there is more that is essentially dramatic in Eliot's early poetry than in his plays. What character in all his plays is as memorable as Prufrock or Apeneck Sweeney or Lil with her false teeth and her contraceptive pills?

The Waste Land, complex structure of parts organized into unity, is completely serious in what it is saying. One cannot well call it a "message," for it is not preaching, but the underlying thought is thus expressed in *Modern Poetry and The Tradition* by Cleanth Brooks: "Life devoid of meaning is death; sacrifice, even the sacrificial death may be life-giving, an awakening to life. The poem occupies itself to a great extent with this paradox." In *The Intent of the Critic*, W. H. Auden considers that "the poem is about the absence of belief and its very unpleasant consequences; it implies throughout a passionate belief in damnation: that to be without belief is to be lost." Similar is the statement by Frederick J. Hoffman:

> *The Waste Land* is not a poem for any one given time; it not merely describes a local circumstance but reveals a universal dilemma. The essential emotions of the poem are the terror and agony that accompany a loss of belief, of the capacity to believe, to enter absolutely into a communication with the spiritual and the moral life.　　(*The Twenties*)

Critics who spend time complaining of the disjointed character of *The Waste Land* would be better critics of this particular poem if they spent more time studying its aesthetic structure and mode of composition. Inasmuch as it is one of the most structured and ordered poems in existence, a critic's complaint of its sudden alternations of mood is merely the critic's self-confessed and self-conferred certificate of incompetence in his profession. But it must be understood, as Eliot himself has said and as Coleridge before him also said, "there is a logic of the imagination as well as a logic of concepts." The organization of *The Waste Land* is aesthetic, not discursive.

The Waste Land has a five-part structure. Part I, "The Burial of the Dead," introduces Waste Land themes and characters, death and fertility cult. Any of the long movements of *The Waste Land* will serve the purpose, but this first movement shows as well as any Eliot's aesthetic organization, similar in theme and countertheme to a musical composition or to the volumes and colors, contrasting and balancing, of a Picasso painting. Particularly brilliant is the insertion of the passage about "looking into the heart of light" and the hyacinth girl between the two quotations from the Wagner opera, *Tristan and Isolde*, the first quotation indicating fresh wind and youthful hope, the second, *Oed' und leer das Meer*, "empty and desolate the sea," a sense of total desolation. The opposition of tonality between passages and the contrasts are masterfully handled.

The Waste Land shows that the waste landers have an insatiable hunger for mutual love, sympathy, and understanding. But in the experiences of human relationship in Parts II and III, there is always a lack, a hunger that is not satisfied. Spiritual love and understanding try to bloom but are strangled for lack of interfeeling and communication. The neurasthenic woman, the "lady of nerves" in Part II, is driven to frenzy by the vacuity of her existence. But her husband or companion is of little assistance; he is too much absorbed in his own subjective feelings. What the poem clearly says is that all our failures are failures of love.

One of the reasons why the Waste Land is waste is that there is a parching lack of significance. The problem of *The Waste Land* is emptiness at the center of existence. The people in it are isolated, each one locked in his prison, like Coriolanus or like the lady of nerves. They may talk, gesture, make noises at each other, and toot horns as at New Year parties, but there is no genuine depth of communication. Each person is locked in the prison cell of the self. The people in *The Waste Land* do not *give*. The world that they inhabit encourages a superficial togetherness; they have a semblance of gaiety when, in the language of the period, they wear "glad rags" or jerk up and down to jazz in the blue, dimly lit cave of a London nightclub.

At the end of the poem is there any hope? One cannot say that the ending is brimming with optimism. The Fisher King, protagonist, is sitting on the shore fishing, and he is perhaps hopeful of catching something (perhaps he will only catch a cold). The arid plain is *behind* him, and he is at least considering setting his lands in order. The man fishing is Adam, or, as Northrup Frye has phrased it in *T. S. Eliot*, "human nature that cannot redeem itself." The way to salvation has been plainly announced, but, as C. M. Bowra says in *The Creative Experiment*, "the final obstacles to the new life demanded by the Thunder are in men themselves." The recalcitrant organ is the human heart.

In his next work, *The Hollow Men* (1925), Eliot touched

the bottom of despair. The epigraph, "Mistah Kurtz—he dead" is from Conrad's *Heart of Darkness* (a novella which meant much to Eliot at this time), and one feels that it is civilization itself whose death announcement is here being made, and the accompanying feeling is that of Kurtz's dying words, "The horror, the horror"—words which Eliot originally wanted to use as epigraph for *The Waste Land*. The hollow men are not only "guys" or "dummies," headpieces filled with straw, to be hanged or burned on Guy Fawkes' Day. They are stuffed shirts, not lost, violent souls, but those who have no faith and no commitment, "behaving as the wind behaves." Perhaps nuclear explosion may be offered as the most suitable representation for the fragmentation of all meaning. Even the Lord's Prayer has been shot and is given to us in desultory pieces.

Eliot's formal adoption of the Anglican faith (that of the Catholic church in England, as he would put it) and British citizenship in 1927 was reflected in the poetic works that followed that event: *Ash-Wednesday*, *The Rock*, and *Murder in the Cathedral*. In *Ash-Wednesday* (1930), surely one of the most disciplined poems in English, perhaps the innermost core of meaning, the central insight, is in the words "Teach us to care and not to care," which are important enough to be first given in Section I and repeated in Section VI. This means that the practice of a kind of unattached attachment, a detachment without total loss of touch towards the things of this world. "Not to care"—that is, not to care too much for them; "to care"—that is, to care enough for the things of this world to perform one's duty for others capably, but to care principally for the things that do not pertain to this world. To care and not to care is a religious paradox of the first importance, and if there were nothing else in it, *Ash-Wednesday* would be of value for this alone.

The crowning work of Eliot's nondramatic poetry is recognized by all to be *Four Quartets* (1943). This work was not, however, originally planned as a unit; "Burnt Norton" was the first to be conceived. The other three quartets came along one by one, until it became clear that the four together were a unified work.

The place names in the titles of the *Four Quartets* may sound strange, but they are all names of places that have been significant in Eliot's personal life or family history. Burnt Norton is the name of a country house in Gloucestershire, where he had an experience of illumination in the late summer of 1934; East Coker is a village in Somerset just south of Yeovil from which his ancestors emigrated to America in the seventeenth century; the Dry Salvages are rocks off the coast of Cape Ann, Massachusetts, remembered by Eliot from summer holidays as a boy; Little Gidding, in Huntingdonshire, visited by Eliot in the spring of 1936, is the site of a lay community founded in the seventeenth century, in fact, an Anglican shrine. In any event, it is a good thing to invoke the spirit of place in poetry; a locus is a good invitation to meditate.

Part of Eliot's great strength is his discipline and his organization. Each quartet, for example, is based on one of the four elements. The element of "Burnt Norton" is air; of "East Coker," the Somerset poem, earth; of "The Dry Salvages," water, both river and sea; finally, of "Little Gidding," fire. Eliot's art is shown by the fact that, though he deals with profound questions of time and eternity, he seldom lets us forget the element: the quivering air of a summer's day in "Burnt Norton," the earth in "East Coker," the rampaging Mississippi River or the raging sea in "The Dry Salvages." In "Little Gidding" purgation by fire, always a favorite theme in Eliot, receives its most ardent treatment in a religious lyric ("The dove descending breaks the air") of an intensity rare in any time and probably unique in ours.

The structure of *Four Quartets* will bear careful examination. The arrangement of the *Quartets* is more complex than it appears at first glance. Each major movement is divided into two halves, so that we have, for instance, "Burnt Norton" I, 1 and 2; "Burnt Norton" II, 1 and 2; and so on. The exception in every quartet is the fourth movement, which is always a lyric and indivisible. Another example of patterned structure is that the first half of the fifth movement is a discussion of a poet's use of language. But this pattern is varied in "Dry Salvages" V, 1, where, instead of the usual linguistic discussion, Eliot sprays his disdain on a number of targets, including Freudian psychoanalysis, spiritual séances, sortilege, and the attempt (the words have a contemporary ring) "to communicate with Mars."

The *Quartets* as poetry are more meditative than anything else he has written. The best philosophical and religious poetry to be found in our language, they are a sustained meditation on the meaning of time in human existence and also on the meaning of time *sub specie aeternitatis*, in its relation to eternity. Time is either redeemed or unredeemed. It is unredeemed if it is viewed in the usual common-sense way as a succession of "nows." In this view, time is unredeemable and it cannot be preserved. This is the pessimistic view of time found in W. H. Auden's "As I Walked Out One Evening":

> *In headaches and in worry*
> *Vaguely life leaks away.*

The "Burnt Norton" meditation ends as it began with a return to the same theme of unredeemed time:

> *Ridiculous the sad waste time*
> *Stretching before and after.*

Eliot's view of time, as it appears from the body of the first quartet, is the opposite of this, however; time is redeemable. One does not have to submit to a sentimental regret for the past as so much water under the bridge or so much that has gone irretrievably down the drain. On the contrary, time may be redeemed and restored to one's present conscious life by viewing the past in a wholly new light and thus "redeeming" it. But with Eliot the supernatural or the eternal is invoked to redeem it. The actual point of the intersection of time with the timeless is the Christic point of time, the mystery of the Incarnation, when the Godhead, or the eternal, took human form. It was then that time as it is ordinarily experienced by human beings was intersected by another dimension of time that is eternal. The mystery, the miracle, was the insertion of the eternal into the temporal; the meeting place was Jesus Christ, both God and man. At particularly significant moments of human experience and human history that intersection of time and the timeless is repeated.

The rose-garden experience in "Burnt Norton" is an experience of a moment of illumination, of a moment when time and the timeless coincide. But for most of us, Eliot is saying, it is impossible to hold on to such moments; all we know is a fitful illumination, "the moment in and out of

time." Only the saints experience such illumination with
any frequency or possess the vision steadily. Although such
moments lift us out of time altogether into a transcendent
region of the mind itself and its own meanings, yet such
experiences can only be remembered in time:

> *To be conscious is not to be in time,*
> *But only in time can the moment in the rose-garden,*
> *The moment in the arbour where the rain beat,*
> *The moment in the draughty church at smokefall*
> *Be remembered; involved with past and future,*
> *Only through time time is conquered.*

Both lines, the initial and the closing one in this passage,
are among the most significant in the *Quartets*. The opening
line, "To be conscious is not to be in time" runs squarely
counter to the ordinary way of looking at things. For most
of us, to be conscious is to be time conscious, is to be *in* time.
For Eliot the reverse is true. To be conscious is to enjoy a
moment of free or higher consciousness of pure apprecia-
tion unattended by time-bound considerations or motives
of profit and loss.

A theme so powerfully sounded in the first quartet will
naturally appear again in later ones. For example, what
becomes important in "East Coker," the earth-bound poem,
is "Not the intense moment / Isolated, with no before and
after, / But a lifetime burning in every moment." In other
words, the lighted moment of emotional intensity is too
elusive. Although one may experience temporary union
with the "still point" in moments of acute mental and emotional awareness, often symbolized by Eliot as "the shaft of
sunlight," final union with the still point may be attained
only by the discipline of the mystic and the saint, earned by

a lifetime of devotion, penetrated by the divine in every moment. In "The Dry Salvages" the theme has one of its greatest statements:

> *But to apprehend*
> *The point of intersection of the timeless*
> *With time, is an occupation for the Saint—*
> *No occupation either, but something given*
> *And taken, in a lifetime's death in love,*
> *Ardour, and selflessness and self-surrender.*
> *For most of us there is only the unattended*
> *Moment, the moment in and out of time,*
> *The distraction fit, lost in a shaft of sunlight,*
> *The wild thyme unseen, or the winter lighting*
> *Or the waterfall, or music heard so deeply*
> *That it is not heard at all, but you are the music*
> *While the music lasts. These are only hints and*
> *   guesses,*
> *Hints followed by guesses; and the rest*
> *Is prayer, observance, discipline, thought and*
> *   action.*
> *The hint half guessed, the gift half understood,*
> *   is Incarnation.*
> *Here the impossible union*
> *Of spheres of existence is actual . . . .*

One of the causes of deepest satisfaction and pleasure in the *Quartets* is the very great sensitiveness and depth of Eliot's response to the arts. Although it is implicit throughout, two places where it is most present are in the passage about the Chinese jar and in another one about listening to music. The words have a matchless dignity, a sense of having arrived, rather than the straining incantation of the Romantics:

Words move, music moves
Only in time; but that which is only loving
Can only die. Words, after speech, reach
Into the silence. Only by the form, the pattern,
Can words or music reach
The stillness, as a Chinese jar still
Moves perpetually in its stillness.

Pattern, meaning order, is a sacred word in Eliot; art for him is order imposed upon existence. The paradox of moving stillness, as in Keats's Grecian urn, is here manifested in arrested movement. But the stillness has reference to the still point, or center of being.

The other passage, which occurs where the theme of the intersection of time with the timeless is introduced (already quoted above) is very brief:

Music heard so deeply
That it is not heard at all, but you are the music
While the music lasts.

The significance of this passage is that a whole phenomenological theory of aesthetic response is embedded in it. What occurs here is the identity between subject and object, between receiver and that which is received, which is the ideal phenomenological state of affairs when a perfectly ordered work of art makes its impact upon viewer or auditor.

It is tempting to divide Eliot's work between poems and plays, and the division is real enough. But underneath the surface of both poems and plays there is "a network of tentacular roots," a system of image and symbol that proves the unity of Eliot's work and integrates it as a single fabric. For example, the symbols of the rose garden, the shaft of sunlight, and the wheel with the still point are found in both poems and plays.

The symbolism of the wheel is absolutely central to any comprehension of Eliot. It is a particularly rich symbol because it includes all of reality, from the still center to the circumference of outer space. The wheel is really a double symbol, for it can refer to both time and the timeless, but it can also refer to action and suffering, with their opposite, peace, at the center. It effects a paradoxical union between action and repose. It has the further advantage for Eliot that it combines the occidental and the oriental mystical traditions. We have both the unmoved mover of Aristotle and Aquinas together with the wheel symbol of Buddhism. The rim of the wheel is *maya,* or illusion; to be bound to the rim is suffering or even torture, rather than freedom or release. Then, too, the symbolism of time is well served by the wheel, for the tire of the wheel symbolizes the temporal, while the axle round which the wheel turns but which itself does not move represents the still point.

A cluster of thought and imagery, which involves the wheel, the still point, action, and suffering, is found in Becket's first important utterance in *Murder in the Cathedral,* when he delivers the following astounding and show-stopping speech (the "they" of the opening words refers to the chorus of Canterbury women):

> *They know and do not know, what it is to act or*
> *   suffer.*
> *They know and do not know that acting is suffering*
> *And suffering is action. Neither does the actor*
> *   suffer*
> *Nor the patient act. But both are fixed*
> *In an eternal action, an eternal patience*

To which all must consent that it may be willed
And which all must suffer that they may will it
That the pattern may subsist, for the pattern is
    the action
And the suffering, that the wheel may turn and
    still
Be forever still.

In *The Third Voice*, Denis Donoghue has commented as follows upon the Archbishop's noble utterance: "When Thomas descants, the play stands still. (When Antony addressed the Roman mob, the play rushed forward.)" The point is forcefully made and well taken. Yet it may be said in Eliot's defense that the Shakespearean theater is much more naturalistic than Eliot's; Eliot is writing a liturgical and ritualistic drama. Becket's opening speech announces the central theme of the play: the anguish involved in bringing the personal will (particularly when the person involved is strong and self-willed) into conformity with God's will, and yet it is precisely here that the central peace is to be found. Implicit in martyrdom is the union of the saint's will with God's will, but it must be a free and willing act of his will, not to his own glory, but for the victory of God's will in the world. The play pursues this theme with undeviating unity.

Eliot in his *The Use of Poetry and the Use of Criticism* has written a brilliant passage on the various levels of meaning in a Shakespeare play. His own play, *Murder in the Cathedral*, is an illustration of a play that has many levels of meaning. But though there are many levels, in the main the play moves upon two planes, with occasional or even constant intersection between them; natural enough, since Incarnation is the world view and the metaphysics undergirding the play as a whole. One plane is that of external action, the plot structure, including the murder, when the Archbishop is celebrating Mass, and on this plane all the action takes place in public or shared time; the other plane is that of interior reality and takes place out of time. When Thomas says, "Human kind cannot bear very much reality," he means that human kind is usually so busy about its affairs that it rarely experiences spiritual reality, nor can it stand very much of it. The action takes place in time, but on another plane it is in the timeless time of the still point.

Eliot is insistent upon the discontinuity of various orders or planes of reality. In *The Idea of a Theater*, Francis Fergusson quotes an introduction that Eliot wrote to the *Pensées of Pascal*:

> Capital . . . is his analysis of the *three orders*: the order of nature, the order of mind, and the order of charity. These three are *discontinuous*; the higher is not implicit in the lower as in an evolutionary doctrine it would be. In this distinction Pascal offers much about which the modern world would do well to think.

Fergusson then turns the passage into a criticism of *Murder in the Cathedral*, saying that just as there is a discontinuity between orders of reality in Eliot, so there is a similar discontinuity between the characters in the play, who never really touch:

> The Chorus would be in the order of nature; the Tempters, Priests and Knights in the order of the mind; and Thomas is the order of charity . . . . Hence the mechanical feel of the play as a whole: the dramatis personae are as discontinuous from each other and from any common world as the parts of a machine.

Theoretically this is well enough, but if the play were as mechanical as Fergusson claims, it would not be as powerful and moving as it is when ably directed and competently acted.

I do not know any play in the modern theater that has more unity than *Murder in the Cathedral*. Nothing in English equals it, unless it is Milton's *Samson Agonistes*, and Milton has far less dramatic sense than Eliot. To find parallels to the unity of *Murder in the Cathedral*, one would have to go back to Sophocles' *Oedipus Rex* or to the *Phèdre* of Racine. It is one of the great plays in the dramatic literature of the world, and easily the greatest of Eliot's plays. Here he was most completely at home with his material.

In his work for the stage Eliot showed a remarkable adaptability. Each play was a new beginning, something quite unattempted before. *Sweeney Agonistes*, with its primitive drumbeat rhythms, was a reaching back to the origin of drama itself. *Murder in the Cathedral* was a strict inquiry into the nature and essence of martyrdom conducted dramatically; it was an *Everyman*, or morality play, centered upon a historical figure. *The Family Reunion* was an adventure into the modern world; its leading character Harry, a modern Orestes, was pursued by Furies, the objectification of a guilty conscience. Essentially it is a Christian existentialist play. It bears a resemblance to Sartre's *The Flies* in this one point, if no other, that the Furies have no power to hurt the hero once he becomes authentic and faces up to them. *The Cocktail Party* again explores the theme of martyrdom, now in a modern setting, but offers the alternative of Christian marriage; as in Greek plays (and this one is modeled on the *Alcestis* of Euripides) the death of the victim Celia, the sainted, the enskied one, is reported by the nuntius, or messenger, Alex. Eliot's next play, *The Confidential Clerk*, is something very new indeed: sacred farce. He has acquired such ease in verse by this time that his verse for the theater is adapted to any tone or level whatever, from the serious to the ridiculous, to even the silly or outright funny. Finally, to crown the series, comes the most human of his plays, *The Elder Statesman*, Eliot's equivalent to Shakespeare's *Tempest* or Sophocles' *Oedipus at Colonus.*

When one looks over Eliot's dramatic achievement as a whole, one finds it impressive. His forging of an infinitely subtle and elastic verse line is a permanent gift to the theater. In the resurrection of the verse play he has outstripped all competitors in English. When one considers his plays thematically, one discovers the truth of a remark by Denis Donoghue: "Eliot's plays are variations on the idea of Holiness, its perversion and its possibility in the modern world." The courage and the integrity with which Eliot has persisted in this theme set him off as remarkable in this irreligious and more and more secular century. Every Eliot play is a spiritual pilgrimage. Whether the character is named Sweeney or Becket or Harry or Celia, the play is always a search for the true self.

One is rather overwhelmed by all this aspiration towards sanctity, but one has to remind oneself that the life of the theater is the life of man in this world. It is Eliot's privilege to turn the theater into a church if he wishes to, but "theater" and "the theatrical" are essentially about human life. One sympathizes, of course, with Eliot's rebellion against naturalistic representation, but one only wishes that he had carried it further and that instead of meekly bowing the knee, so that, outwardly at least, *The Elder Statesman* is indistinguishable from a conventional play, he had been bold enough to smash the conventional frame altogether. Eliot's drama has a certain religious intensity; it is always distinguished; his plays bear close textual study and are invariably rewarding. His dramatic muse is a gray-eyed Athena, a chaste goddess of wisdom; she seems never to have known the passions of the flesh. Eliot's great mistake as a playwright is that of turning his back upon the world. If one is to renounce the world *in toto*, one may as well renounce the theater, too. Eliot's world is protected, it is upper class, and though, indeed, in *Murder in the Cathedral* there is a gesture towards understanding the way ordinary people feel (the women of Canterbury) and an acknowledgment of the quivering horror that may and does occur in real life ("the torn girl by the millstream"), yet nevertheless this is reported to us inside a cathedral as a rumor from the outside, and the words, the cold words, rebound hollowly within the Gothic vaults. To be sure, this criticism requires modification, for in his later plays, including *The Cocktail Party* and from there on, he turned increasingly toward the world, without abandoning his otherworldly aim.

By comparison with the great achievement of the European theater represented by Beckett, Sartre, Genêt, and Ionesco, the theater of Eliot, while weighty and considerable, appears tamer, less experimental, less original, and also less representative of our time. Eliot has worn his ecclesiastical mufflers; he has not faced the cold east wind of the absurd. His later plays are comparable to the unexceptionable but unexciting Christian plays of Gabriel Marcel. Indeed, when one considers the three defenders of the Roman Catholic religion in the theater, Claudel, Marcel, and Eliot, one has to conclude that the devil's advocate, Sartre, in plays like *No Exit* and *The Devil and the Good Lord*, has the better of the day, not only theatrically but morally also. For one could argue, and with good reason, that Sartre is a more stimulating moralist than Eliot, in spite of the undoubted greatness of *Murder in the Cathedral*.

Every age, I suppose, gets the epic or the major poem that it deserves. The heroic age got the *Iliad*. The Roman age got the *Aeneid*. Our age got *The Waste Land* (it has all the weight of an epic), its own appropriate epitaph. Matthew Arnold was physician to an iron age. In Eliot's day the iron had corroded; a civilization was eaten away. Eliot is hardly to be envied. He did what he could. He did much better than Pound in "Mauberley" which is comparatively crude in its attack. Eliot felt the pulse of the age, presented it with its own fever chart, and put its thermometer in its mouth. He accurately diagnosed a disease that had gone beyond malaise. It must be said, too, that he had such a perfect bedside manner that one felt confidence in his diagnosis.

Eliot did not reform the taste of the age, for it had no taste to be reformed. He gave taste to an age that was tasteless and graceless. He simply referred it, by slipping a century or two, to its own great heritage, its own past. He taught a whole generation, not how to be sensitive (they were already that), but to be sensitive to certain things, to be sensitive in a certain way. He articulated their sensitivity. He was the conscience of his age, as Camus was of a later age. He taught his age to be aware of itself; through him a whole generation learned that it was hollow.

Eliot's work is at its best when he deals with the now in its presentness. His phenomenological apprehension of reality—his just and accurate recording of what the experiencing consciousness experiences when it is vis-à-vis whatever it is that it experiences—and the uncompromising honesty with which this is done marks Eliot's poetry at its best. This, together with his concision of phrasing, his dramatic gift, is essentially why he is to be considered a great poet.

Yet Eliot's life work, at least for this reader and probably for many others, is in part valid and in part not. He paid a high price, too high a price, perhaps, for his orthodoxy, because he turned his back upon the religion of the future and sought order and salvation either in the past or in some atemporal realm outside the circle of realty altogether. A very great man (one of the greatest, equal, perhaps, to Virgil or Dante in his poetic gifts), but not even the greatest of men can arrest flow or the forward movement of man towards new integrations of experience. One could wish that he had been more open to change, more willing, as was Dietrich Bonhoeffer, to rethink Christian faith in a radical way.

No matter what critical objections may be raised, however, Eliot's work has a unique quality not to be found in many of our writers—not in Chaucer or Shakespeare or Milton, in none of our Romantic poets, not even Keats for all his ardor, and certainly not in Arnold. It is a searching for the spiritual center, for within the dramatic text one always finds the search for integrity, and it expresses itself, at moments, as an unstained spiritual radiance. Although one may find a greater warmth in Shakespeare and a more universal understanding of the human heart, one will nowhere find the steady, unwavering emphasis upon the still point that one finds in Eliot. His work has a unity and a philosophical profundity unequaled in English. The same distinction lights up everything he wrote, whether it is *Four Quartets*, which ranks among the major poetry of our time, or something extremely minor like *The Cultivation of Christmas Trees*: from first to last the same religious spirit informs the whole. Even the early poems, before his conversion, express a sense of outrage at the lack of religion in the world. Paradoxically, though no one more sternly forbade the personal experience in poetry unless it found its objective correlative or was transmuted into art, everything he wrote bears his personal stamp and has his own inimitable personal rhythm. So it happened to Eliot, the invisible poet, who with smooth precision strove to iron himself out of his verse.

When one considers the four founding fathers of modern Anglo-American poetry—Pound, Stevens, Williams, and Eliot—one notices that each of these markedly individual poets has a dominant concern. Although Ezra Pound has his aesthetic concern (a Venetian dock, lucid water lapping on white marble gondola stairs seems to be his emblem of civilization), his deepest concern of all, in his quixotic and archaic way, is with economic justice. Wallace Stevens' central concern is with aesthetic honesty. William Carlos Williams, less precious in his aesthetic concern than Stevens, is primarily concerned with people and their lives in the industrial city. Eliot's ultimate concern is with discipline and with belief, with the removal of aridity by the living water of the word.

His position is secure, for he belongs, together with Yeats and Rilke, to the triumvirate of the most influential twentieth-century poets. He is assured of a place in history and in literature, as long as there is a history and there is a literature. As things are today, this is no great guarantee of permanence; one can but hope. His achievement remains, even though some day on our contaminated planet it may be that no one will be there to appreciate it, and though "The worlds revolve like ancient women / Gathering fuel in vacant lots."

WILLIAM FAULKNER

by Frederick J. Hoffman

Two DATES seem important in the recent history of William Faulkner's work: on July 6, 1962, he died of a heart attack in Oxford, Mississippi, at the age of sixty-five; and in November, 1950, he was awarded the 1949 Nobel Prize for literature. The point of relationship between these dates has to do with a general rush (after each, and between them) toward reappraisals and the identification of his work with the wider world, with the nature of man. In general, critics, and Faulkner as well, tried both to import and to export meaning in terms of his creative work. That the critical evaluation of Faulkner has increased vastly is testified to in recent check lists; foreign critics have been especially active. All of this may just be an elaborate obituary; in the future we may just have a soberer and a sparer retrospective look at the reputation.

A fact that no student of Faulkner will fail to have noticed is that he himself has aided and abetted the general view; he seems anxious to have himself established as, above all, a profound writer, engaged in establishing and in dramatizing the verities within a human context. James Meriwether, in the preface to a recent collection of Faulkner's essays, speeches, and public letters (that there should be enough of them for a collection is in itself a phenomenon), writes of his "mature achievement in the field of nonfiction prose." The maturity would appear to me to be almost entirely a matter of chronology. The years after the Nobel Prize were characterized by an earnest push toward sainthood, of the editorial cast. Faulkner suddenly became a man of many public words.[1] The words are themselves of two kinds: self-analysis, looking backward upon his achievement and appraising it, and public statement, sometimes relating his perspective on his work but often on issues of the human story. Fifty-three of the items in Meriwether's collection of sixty-five are from the post-Nobel time, the last twelve years of his life.

The importance of all this for a summary of Faulkner's importance may be gathered from some such generality as this, which I offer as a guideline for attending to this essay: that in the years from 1929 to 1950 he was mainly preoccupied with creating his world and its creatures, his "little postage stamp of native soil"; that, for the most part, after 1950 he busied himself endowing his past and present work—and above all himself—with a dignity and a significance that were largely imported from the outside; and that there was a comparable change in styles, manner of presentation, and rhetoric. There are important exceptions to what I have

---

[1] Aside from book reviews and a few public letters, the only items prior to 1950 were the famous introduction to the Modern Library Edition of Sanctuary (1932) and the "Funeral Sermon" for Mammy Caroline Burr (1940). The latter was given on the occasion of the death of Faulkner's favorite Negro servant, believed to be the model of Dilsey of *The Sound and the Fury* (1929).

said: fine insights and presentation in *The Town* (1957) and *The Mansion* (1959) and especially in the non-dramatic passages of *Requiem for a Nun*; comedy in the best Faulkner tradition in *The Reivers* (1962). These would surely testify that Faulkner was capable of continuing strength as a literary artist, of a commitment to the requirements of his art. But an increasing burden of his work since 1950 has the quality of the public stance, the positioning of the wise man who has suddenly discovered he is wise, and there are sometimes unfortunate results for the writing generally. Unlike Thomas Mann, André Malraux, Albert Camus, and Ignazio Silone, Faulkner was not a precise or an imaginative intellectual; he did not give abstractions or generalities with a skill of language that might have made them come alive on the page, and he was liable to end, more frequently than not, either in sentimentality or in stale cliché.

There is some doubt that this change is necessarily a consequence of the Nobel award: *post hoc, ergo propter hoc.* Yet the facts of literary history point to the strong possibility. His time of greatness (1929–48, or from *The Sound and the Fury* to *Intruder in the Dust*) yielded abundant evidence of his natural talent—not just that of an untutored genius, because he was intensely concerned to exploit his talent, but a skill and a power that were the envy of all modern writers of fiction. The extravagances of rhetoric matched (as his "voice" improved the occasions of) the dramatic and literary necessities. Above all, he was aware of himself as creator bringing a world and its people into being, in the best Balzacian sense of the phrase. In an interview with Jean Stein for *Paris Review*, he put it this way:

Beginning with *Sartoris* (1929) I wrote for the sake of writing because it was fun. Beginning with *Sartoris* I discovered that my own little postage stamp of native soil was worth writing about and that I would never live long enough to exhaust it, and that by sublimating the actual into the apocryphal I would have complete liberty to use whatever talent I might have to its absolute top. It opened up a gold mine of other people, so I created a cosmos of my own. I can move these people around like God, not only in space but in time too. The fact that I have moved my characters around in time successfully, at least in my own estimation, proves to me my own theory that time is a fluid condition which has no existence except in the momentary avatars of individual people . . . .

This is a fascinating statement, which deserves full commentary. It is Faulkner looking back upon a remarkable career; whether it accurately defines his feeling in 1929, when the career was ahead of him, we can only conjecture. But the realization of an accessible world is there in all its strength, as is the sense of the creative power. By "sublimating the actual into the apocryphal" (that is, by recreating the real world of Faulkner's Oxford, Mississippi, and environs into the imagined world of Jefferson and Yoknapatawpha County), he was able to dominate and control it and to create within it, with remarkable results. The decision to write about the country he best knew, to present what he knew in a multiplicity of detail, released his creative energies, so that he could replace his acquaintances with reintegrated creatures, whom he could maneuver into any number of scenic and dramatic situations. The possibilities were nearly inexhaustible, and the prospect of the last book, the "Doomsday Book" as he called it, did not seem likely. In fact, in the year of his death *The Reivers* suggested that he could have had many more areas of exploration, had he lived.

Whatever the effect of the Nobel award, we can say that two kinds of rhetoric had always been possible within Faulkner's work; the award and the consequent public revelation of Faulkner as an artist of great talent tended to force the public rhetoric, as opposed to the rhetoric of self-containment, of creative self-sufficiency, which he had largely demonstrated up to then. The issue was a delicate one: Faulkner could have, at any time, abandoned the sufficient uses of his style and produced sermons instead of stories; but for the most part, because of a tendency to shun the glare of public acclaim and to stay within range of his created world, he succeeded in avoiding the temptation. He always possessed a rich, dense, heavy, and elaborate style, which led to a lavish syntax, remarkably involved sentences and paragraphs, and a luxuriant jungle of adjectives, adverbs, and qualifying phrases and clauses. Except in a few examples of the shorter forms, Faulkner's work has always been rich and in danger of becoming excessive. Yet, for the most part, he held the talent within bounds, in fact utilized it to give many of his characters a depth of consciousness that they could not themselves have demonstrated. This added dimension is described most usefully as Faulkner's "voice" in an essay by Sister Kristin Morrison:

> Faulkner . . . frequently represents throughout his work not the literal mind-voice but a heightened voice: a voice that is rooted in the mind of the character, a voice that issues from that mind and yet is not bound by the limits of intelligence and insensibility which that mind has by nature, a voice heightened to perception and articulation of which the mind itself is incapable.

Sister Kristin goes on to suggest, "Such a heightening is similar to the phenomenon of possession of a human medium by a transcendent spirit: the medium speaks, his voice possessed by the spirit, speaks things of which he is himself perhaps unaware, even incapable of understanding; yet it is his own voice issuing from his person, his voice made oracular and transcendent." Perhaps this last metaphor is a bit unfortunate, as though Faulkner were God breathing the spirit through his creatures. The analogy is not too much out of the question, however; though I should like to say that Faulkner's characters, rather than being possessed by him, are empowered by him to make their obsessions overtly clear and notable. I think this interpretation also puts us within reach of a plausible understanding of the great temptation that must have haunted Faulkner throughout his career, that became obvious in the last years of his life, especially in *A Fable* (1954), in which what was implicit in the early work became overworked and belabored.

Faulkner's characters are almost always a demented, overworked, and overstrained lot. On the surface they are often very ordinary human beings, with limited powers of expression; yet, in the voice of their author, they express profundities that are literally beyond their own power to bring to the surface, that *require* the help of Faulkner's voice to bring to light. The tall convict of *The Wild Palms* (1939), for example, has been sent out from the Parchman prison farm to rescue a pregnant woman from the flooding waters of the Mississippi. He goes about his duties in what appears to be a matter-of-fact way, yet Faulkner indicates to us an inarticulate though powerful philosophical disposition toward the world about him. The Mississippi River symbolizes for him all of the calamitous risks brought about by a failure of restraints, and ultimately we see that land (the land of the prison farm especially) is a sign of safety, of inhibition and control, and water its opposite, which he hates and fears. Faulkner presents us with the high and deep comedy of a man imprisoned for life who because of flood waters has an opportunity to become a "free" man but eventually chooses against the idea of freedom. Here, in the passage following, the rhetorical possibilities of this situation are given in a way he must have felt but of course could not himself have used:

> It was mud he lay upon, but it was solid underneath, it was earth, it would not move; if you fell upon it you broke your bones against its incontrovertible passivity sometimes but it did not accept you substanceless and enveloping and suffocating, down and down and down; it was hard at times to drive a plow through, it sent you spent, weary, and cursing its light-long insatiable demands back to your bunk at sunset at times but it did not snatch you violently out of all familiar knowing and sweep you thrall and impotent for days against any returning . . . .

This is all brilliantly apt; yet we know that the special vocabulary and syntax are Faulkner's gift to the occasion, though there is no violation of the narrative proprieties. It is the responsibility of the novelist to see beyond his character (though not in a way different from his). The qualities of the tall convict's own manner of articulation are given in the next two sentences, printed in italics as a sign of the change in manner:

> *I dont know where I am and I dont reckon I know the way back to where I want to go,* he thought. *But at least the boat has stopped long enough to give me a chance to turn it around.*

144

This colorless, uninflected language represents the naturalistic character, as the following remark near the end of his story suggests the limits within which he had regarded his task at its completion:

> "All right," the other said. "Yonder's your boat, and here's the woman. But I never did find that bastard on the cottonhouse."

The passages quite suitably describe the range of Faulkner's rhetoric when it is functioning within the limits, both actual and extended, of his characters. In fact, his best fiction offers us a brilliant succession of such moments: the subject is itself relatively limited; his characters are country folk with a wry and amusing sense of the world around them, or desperate persons trying to find a form of assertion through either acts or sufferings or a succession of the two, or persons who obey certain inherited rules of order but rarely spend time explaining why they are doing so.[2] A quiet lot: yet beneath the surface of their laconic communication, emotions seethe. It is largely up to Faulkner to give us the real measure of their sensibilities, without going too far himself or allowing his rhetoric to distract from the characterizations.

I should like, in the remainder of this essay, to do two things: first, to show how, in the work from 1929 to 1950, Faulkner almost always succeeded in giving his characters rhetorical assistance, and in so doing, encouraged and enhanced the narrative; second, to describe in a few cases how the rhetoric got away from him, at least partly because he

2 There are, of course, certain big talkers in his novels: Gavin Stevens, for one, V. K. Ratliff, and Jason Richmond Compson, father of Quentin and Candace. The talking, however, is usually carefully distinguished from the expressions of feeling, as though too much erudition and too heavy a style were somehow a violation of decorum.

ignored his characters in his desire to speak not for them but for himself. I am limiting myself to what I believe are the works that led to and away from the Nobel Prize; that is, the novels that influenced the award committee and those after 1950 that seemed to have been influenced by the rhetoric of the occasion.

Perhaps the great masterpieces of controlled style are *The Sound and the Fury* (1929) and *As I Lay Dying* (1930), but these are special instances because they are in large part composed in terms of the interior monologues of involved persons. Yet the achievement is a double one: the characters reveal themselves and at the same time advance the narrative; they are at once personages and narrators, and Faulkner is obliged to attend to both of their functions. In *The Sound and the Fury* we are offered three inside views of the events of the Compson family from 1898 to the Easter week end of 1928. These are followed by a conventional narrative section, but it too is richly informed (in the manner in which Henry James informed his novels) by a comprehending moral consciousness, that of the Negro woman, Dilsey. Section I is quite clearly to be understood as the representation of an idiot son who is quite incapable of verbalizing at all; so it must be claimed not only that Faulkner is verbalizing for him, but also that he is carefully aware at all times of Benjy's limitations and avoids giving him more of a mind than he actually possesses. This does not mean that Benjy is without opinions or a moral judgment, only that they must be represented largely on the level of sensations. Even occasionally sophisticated language is communicated with the understanding that it exists in Benjy's memory of the past; in other words, he sometimes reports words as though they were things, the shape and flavor of which are communicated through the years.

The circumstances of Quentin's report are radically different. Money gained by the sale of Benjy's pasture has enabled him to go to Harvard, but within the day, at the end of his monologue, he commits suicide. While Benjy's monologue is dominated by simplicities, Quentin's is complex in syntax and allusion. Nevertheless, they have their similarities: both minds concentrate upon their sister Caddy; both depend morally upon her virtue; both are shocked into violent acts by an awareness that she has lost her virginity; both wish a stable, a morally fixed world, and are willing to act to retain it; but both fail, and they end dismally, one in death and the other in the state institution for the feeble-minded. Faulkner meets the terms of Benjy's and Quentin's minds beautifully and handles Jason with a sense of the wild humor and complex irony so often encountered in his work:

> The first sane Compson since before Culloden [he called Jason in an appendix for *The Portable Faulkner*] and (a childless bachelor) hence the last. Logical rational contained and even a philosopher in the old stoic tradition: thinking nothing whatever of God one way or the other and simply considering the police and so fearing and respecting only the Negro woman, his sworn enemy since his birth . . . .

Perhaps the turn from interior monologue to third-person narration in Section IV benefits from the stylistic restrictions that the styles of Sections I through III have imposed on the reader. In any case, as Mrs. Vickery has said, "We finally emerge from the closed world of the Compson Mile into the public world as represented by Jefferson . . . ." As one of many consequences, we have a firsthand view of the ways in which the Compson world has diminished, as well as a rewarding impression of the true stature of Dilsey, whose portrait in the opening paragraphs of Section IV has set standards for all time in profound characterization. Here once again the voice of Faulkner plays upon the characterization, offering us insights that the subject could scarcely give in the spirit and depth Faulkner has provided.

> She had been a big woman once but now her skeleton rose, draped loosely in unpadded skin that tightened again upon a paunch almost dropsical, as though muscle and tissue had been courage or fortitude which the days or the years had consumed until only the indomitable skeleton was left rising like a ruin or a landmark above the somnolent and impervious guts . . . .

The consummate skill of complex narration in *The Sound and the Fury* is almost matched in *As I Lay Dying*. Following these two novels, Faulkner experimented with other forms of controlled narration. *Light in August* (1932) is a mixture of violence and quiet; the spirit of Lena Grove helps to keep the novel from falling over the edge of sheer anger and terror. Once again Faulkner must assist in giving significance and depth to characters who would otherwise be quite incapable of giving articulation to their inner intensities. This is true of a number of them, but of none so much as Joe Christmas, the strange, weirdly turned-in orphan who tries to solve the problems, moral and racial, of a suspected (but not an actual) black heritage. The beginning of chapter six is an obvious example of this use of voice.

Memory believes before knowing remembers. Believes long-

148

er than recollects, longer than knowing even wonders. Knows remembers believes a corridor in a big long garbled cold echoing building of dark red brick soot-bleakened by more chimneys than its own, set in a grassless cinderstrewn-packed compound surrounded by smoking factory purlieus and enclosed by a ten foot steel-and-wire fence like a penitentiary or a zoo.

The corridor of memory helps point out to the reader that the past is as it is reconstructed in Christmas' memory, as of the time he murders Joanna Burden. So we not only see the act of murder in a pattern of temporal succession, we also sense in it a causal pattern, comprehending not only the act but the reasons why it is inevitable. Hence, the succession of verbs, "knows, remembers, believes," helps to define a process of Christmas' slowly coming aware of why he must commit the act of murder. As Sister Kristin has pointed out, the rhetoric of Faulkner's presentation of Christmas follows two methods, that of Joe's interior mind and feelings and that of exterior points of view:

First introduced in the voices of others, Joe is described there as a cruel, incomprehensible creature; only after the reader has been made to think this of him does any interior view emerge, and it is in this interior view (in his own heightened voice) that he becomes progressively more amenable to sympathy.

Not only do the interior and external views complement one another, but they make possible one of the remarkable examples of a character living in both past and present. Our awareness of him as a murderer precedes in narrative sequence our understanding (through the journey into various aspects of his past) of him as a person; and time past influences time present steadfastly, beginning with chapter six. The move into the past is preceded by the statement, at the end of chapter five, "*Something is going to happen. Something is going to happen to me.*" The "something" has already happened, or at least we are aware of a happening, though we do not know its full psychological depths until we have come to know Christmas in terms of himself, and this knowledge must come from a view within and a look backward.

We may say that in *Light in August*, Faulkner offers us two safeguards against any display of demonstrative rhetoric. He has stayed within Christmas' consciousness (though, as in other cases, he must support it through his own voice), and he has forced us to see the reason for the murder by examining that act developmentally. Something of the same perspective is used in the characterization of Gail Hightower and Joanna Burden (though, as in the case of Quentin Compson, the rhetoric is more complex and studded with symbols peculiar to their characters); in fact, it is only in the simple characters, the persons who do not suffer from agonies of conscience, doubt, or fear, that the past does not seem to be needed. The next great novel, *Absalom, Absalom!* (1936) presents a similar structure of past-working-upon-present; in this case, however, the pattern is matched by a strenuous activity of present-working-on-past. Generally, we may say that the closest we come to a real present is 1909; it is the time of a climactic event (the house at Sutpen's Hundred burns to the ground, destroying Henry, the last Sutpen heir) as well as a time of assessment. The latter is conducted by the Quentin Compson of *The Sound and the Fury* and his roommate, Shreve McCannon, in the "iron New England dark" of their Harvard dormitory room.

Quentin and Shreve are only the last two persons who try
to put the story of Thomas Sutpen together. The first is Rosa
Coldfield, who in 1866 had been insulted by Sutpen (who
tried to make her agree to live with him, on the risk that if
she bore him a son he would marry her). The wizened little
woman, who has lived out her years nursing her wounded
ego, offers her version of "that demon" to Quentin before he
goes to Harvard. That Rosa's view of Sutpen suffers from
her rage is obvious from the beginning; once again we are
given the worst view of a man and then asked to modify it
in the light of additional evidence. Only this time we are
never entirely sure, since (except for Sutpen's own talk to
Quentin's grandfather, which is strangely isolated and
polite in its rhetoric) the subject matter of the novel is
never really presented from the inside but is only invoked
from a number of external positions. All we can say is that
none of them gives us the full view of Thomas Sutpen; if
we come to know anyone well, it is Quentin Compson, who
takes to heart the story of Sutpen and his rejection of family.
In the end, the fable of Sutpen is confused with Quentin's
own ambivalent relationship to the South. When McCannon asks, "Why do you hate the South?"

"I dont hate it," Quentin said, quickly, at once, immediately;
"I dont hate it," he said. *I dont hate it* he thought, panting
in the cold air, the iron New England dark; *I dont. I dont! I
dont hate it! I dont hate it!*

Absalom, Absalom! is a masterful work in the maneuver-
ing of point of view and time, the object of which is to place
the legend of a warped and distorted vision in a dramatic
setting. The setting is southern, as we know Quentin is, but
Faulkner has several times gone on record for the universal

importance of his locale, most notably in the interview with Jean Stein:

> I like to think of the world I created as being a kind of keystone in the universe; that, as small as that keystone is, if it were ever taken away, the universe itself would collapse....

The ambition here articulated is neither more nor less than that of giving his work a human meaning. That is, he would hope to preserve the particular slope and slant of his world, but he would also hope that his people are not freaks and that they have meaning for the larger world.

There was no sharp change. Faulkner did not awaken the day after his Stockholm address and decide to write differently. Nevertheless, a shift in meaning did occur. He became more interested in his heroes in terms of what they were typically, what they represented. The style sometimes changes, from the accommodating voice I have illustrated to the spokesman. In other words, his heroes sometimes took over for him, in the manner of the country preacher seeking to infer universal meanings from a recent event. One example of this process occurred as early as 1948, in *Intruder in the Dust*. Here, in chapter seven, Gavin Stevens, who had been around before in the fiction but had never quite taken over from his author, begins to enunciate and pontificate, in such a way as to make even the young boy, Chick Mallison, embarrassed with him. It is interesting to see that the message is preceded by a significant change in description of landscape. Speaking of the ritual that should be characteristic of the countryside on a week day, Faulkner describes "the land's living symbol—a formal group of ritual almost mystic significance identical and monotonous as milestones tying the county-seat to the county's ultimate rim as milestones would: the beast the plow and the man integrated in one foundationed into the frozen wave of their furrow tremendous with effort yet at the same time vacant of progress . . . ."

The rhetoric is not much different from that of chapter one of *Light in August* published some sixteen years earlier:

> Behind Lena Grove the four weeks, the evocation of *far*, is a peaceful corridor paved with unflagging and tranquil faith and peopled with kind and nameless faces and voices . . . through which she advanced in identical and anonymous and deliberate wagons as though through a succession of creakwheeled and limpeared avatars, like something moving forever and without progress across an urn.

The style is similar, but the novels are structured differently; the description of Lena's progress from Alabama to Mississippi is not the setting for any editorial remarks, while the pattern of the farming ritual is just that.

We are some distance from the rhetoric of the famous Stockholm address, which contains its own sources of rhetorical self-sufficiency. The very form (uncreative and direct) allows for the most extreme kinds of stylistic indulgence:

> [The writer] must teach himself that the basest of all things is to be afraid; and, teaching himself that, forget it forever, leaving no room in his workshop for anything but the old verities and truths of the heart, the old universal truths lacking which any story is ephemeral and doomed—love and honor and pity and pride and compassion and sacrifice.

Having established these humanistic verities as the groundwork of his aesthetic, Faulkner states his own beliefs:

I believe that man will not merely endure: he will prevail. He is immortal, not because he alone among creatures has an inexhaustible voice, but because he has a soul, a spirit capable of compassion and sacrifice and endurance.

It is not coincidence that Faulkner should have published *Requiem for a Nun* (1951) and *A Fable* (1954) in a sequence after the Nobel award. The former presents Gavin Stevens in the special role of moral and humanist "saint," at work on the task of reforming Temple Drake:

What we are trying to deal with now is injustice. Only truth can cope with that. Or love . . . . Call it pity then. Or simple honor, honesty, or a simple desire for the right to sleep at night.

Although *Requiem* is still concerned with Yoknapatawpha County, *A Fable* is totally removed from it. Concerning it, Irving Howe offered this evaluation:

Neither quite a fable nor a novel, an allegory nor a representation, *A Fable* is an example of the yearning so common to American writers for a "big book," a *summa* of vision and experience, a final spelling-out of the wisdom of the heart . . . . *A Fable*, one regretfully concludes, is still another of those "distinguished" bad books that flourish in America.

Although this is a scolding Faulkner may have deserved, one finds a more reasoned criticism in Mrs. Vickery's remark, that in *A Fable*, Faulkner "subdues the particular and therefore unique aspects of his situation and characters and eliminates that profusion of detail which creates the illusion of reality for Jefferson and its inhabitants . . . ." The problem is, as ever, one of the kinds and the distribution of rhetoric. There are many evidences of a melodramatic posing against the vices and imperfections of the world. The mob in the new dispensation is a form of protoplasm, capable of eventually becoming an entity in one of two ways: by order of authority or by appeals to free will. The danger is that it will solidify according to orders; and the corporal's heroism consists in his being an example for it to follow, a man who will not surrender his individuality. Truth depends upon one heroic assertion; if it is forthcoming, man will endure, and he will prevail.

In the exchange between the corporal and the marshal, the full conflict is joined. Both agree that "man and his folly" will endure and prevail, but they have differing reasons. The marshal maintains that man is a tough, rapacious creature and will therefore survive any monstrous occasion: rapacity, like poverty, "takes care of its own. Because it endures, not even because it is rapacity but because man is man, enduring and immortal; enduring not because he is immortal but immortal because he endures . . . ." The rhetoric is supported by the narrative line itself; while the corporal is never called Jesus Christ, many indications suggest the parallel, and it appears to be intended with great seriousness, despite the fact that *A Fable* cannot ultimately be called an allegory, but only a suggestive tale pointing to a modern adaptation of the Christ figure. In the temptation scene he is offered, not control of the world or its pleasures, but, simply, life, the value of "simply breathing."

Faulkner has said that Christianity is not necessarily true, but that, since it is a commonly possessed heritage, it becomes a part of the material to which an artist has access when he creates. But in *A Fable* the rhetoric takes over from the narrative and, in so doing, devalues it. There is a certain exhilaration, at the beginning, over the magnitude of Faulkner's conception, and a continuing interest in the ways in which he tries to realize it. But it is regrettably true that the heaviness (as well as the vagueness) of Faulkner's purpose provides us eventually with a wearisome text. The corporal is neither God nor man. If he is anything at all, he is entirely man, and his providing a humanistic example is quite unconvincing because there is no genuine significance in his acts. This failure comes partly from Faulkner's dogmatic anxiety to remove the figure from theological implications of the Trinity; he thus deprives him of much of the incentive toward belief, and his acts become aberrant and gratuitous. There is a curious flattening out of the characterization, as contrasted with the depth and dimension of *The Sound and the Fury, Light in August,* and other works of the time of genius. It is almost as though it is possible to reduce a person's achievement by telling him too often that he is a great artist.

It would be an unfair and a distorted view of Faulkner the artist if I were to leave his career at the production of 1954. He did, after all, produce *The Town, The Mansion,* and *The Reivers.* The first of these is marred by a needlessly complicated scheme of narration, but there are many intensely good scenes in *The Mansion,* and *The Reivers* is a minor comic masterpiece. We shall have to assume that the Nobel award was given him for the accomplishments leading up to it; that, in his nonfictional prose his style was too nakedly abstract to be of much use (in other words, that he was capable of complex representation only when he was preoccupied with the "cosmos of [his] own"); and, finally, that *A Fable* must be admired as a strange, eccentric masterpiece in the pursuit of abstract ideas through hundreds of pages that scarcely ever come alive. The award came at the right time; it honored a great artist, and he has certainly justified the Nobel committee's choice far more than many other artists whom it has picked have ever done.

ERNEST HEMINGWAY

by Ken Moritz

IF IN THIRTY YEARS they have not succeeded in reforming the present system they will infallibly relapse into barbarism," said Alfred Nobel, prophecying what the twentieth century portended if men were not sufficiently bright or frightened by the power of his invention to leave it alone. From the debris of this relapse into barbarism after the Edwardian moment, which had looked out optimistically at the high promise of the twentieth century, Ernest Hemingway created a powerful and compelling fictional world which won the 1954 Nobel Prize for Literature "for his powerful, style-forming mastery of the art of modern narration, as most recently evinced in *The Old Man and the Sea*." His account of Santiago, the old fisherman who had gone eighty-four days without a fish, only to sail out too far, catch the biggest fish of his life, and see it destroyed by sharks before he could reach port, had been published in 1952 in *Life* magazine and had received high critical praise.

Honoring Hemingway at the December 10 ceremony in Stockholm, Anders Oesterling, permanent secretary of the

Swedish Academy, conceded that "Hemingway's earlier writings displayed brutal, cynical and callous signs which may be considered at variance with the Nobel Prize requirements for a work of ideal tendencies." However, a "heroic pathos" helped balance this deficiency, and it seemed to others that nowhere was this virtue more strongly apparent than in *The Old Man*, a simple work without complexity or complication whose ideal tendencies would have been immediately apparent to and approved by that late nineteenth-century idealist, Alfred Nobel himself. "But on the other hand," Oesterling continued, "he also possesses a heroic pathos which forms the basic element of his awareness of life, a manly love of danger and adventure, with a natural admiration of every individual who fights the good fight in a world of reality overshadowed by violence and death." The central theme of courage could be seen in "the bearing of one who is put to the test and who steels himself to meet the cold cruelty of existence without by so doing repudiating the great and generous moments." Finally, Hemingway tells the truth. "He is one of the great writers of our time, one of those who, honestly and undauntedly, reproduces the genuine features of the hard countenance of the age."

He had been seriously considered for the 1953 award, but the Academy postponed giving him the prize in favor of the aged Churchill. Later, when it was thought that Hemingway had died in the African air crashes of January, 1954, several Academy members expressed regret at the delay. His closest competitor was Icelandic author Haldor Laxness, who won the prize the next year. Among others considered were Paul Claudel, Albert Camus, and Ezra Pound.

Two or three weeks before the October 28 announcement, Mary Hemingway recalls, the Swedish minister to various Latin-American countries called Hemingway for an appointment at Finca Vigia, his home outside Havana. Guessing what the news would be, Mary toasted Hemingway, but out of caution he refused to join her, preferring to wait for confirmation. A week before the public announcement, the elegant gold medal was bestowed on Hemingway at a simple, private ceremony. "We had," Mary wrote, "a short exchange of speeches, the Swedish Minister and his wife and a few friends standing around in our library, and afterwards one of those sparkling, singing, gay, four-hour luncheon parties with ten or twelve at a table, which happened consistently at the Finca. The Swedish diplomat's pretty wife fell in love with Ernest, as all smart women did, and the line of empty wine bottles in the pantry grew longer. When our guests left there was barely time before dark for our half-mile evening swim in the pool."

It had been a bad year for the Hemingways, and although the award was very good news, its effect was to destroy Hemingway's jealously guarded privacy and to interrupt his working habits. The award came late, for he was moving, as a visitor noted, "into the twilight of his life. He was fifty-five but looked older, and was trying to mend a ruptured kidney, a cracked skull, two compressed and one cracked vertebra, and bad burns suffered in the crash of his airplane in the Uganda bush the previous winter."

On January 23 and 24 he and Mary had crashed twice near Murchison Falls, first in a Cessna 180 and next in the DeHavilland Rapide that was to have rescued them, but burned on takeoff. Hemingway's Spanish doctor had said, "You should have died immediately." The injuries received were added to the others that Hemingway had sustained all over the world in his concern as writer to be up front in the major cockpits of violence in our time. His first big wound—one which was to have a profound influence on his work—occurred on the night of July 8, 1918, at Fossalta di Piave on the Italian front in World War I when, as a volunteer ambulance driver, he had his knee shot away. "I died then," he said. From his right leg 237 fragments of steel were removed. He had an extraordinary capacity for absorbing punishment. He was in three serious automobile wrecks, was shot through both feet, both knees, both arms, both hands, and the scrotum, and was wounded in the head six times. Because he was "too beat-up" from his injuries, his doctor had refused to let him go to Stockholm, the Venice of the north, to make the traditional acceptance speech and receive the prize. His prepared address was read in Stockholm Town Hall by the American ambassador, John Cabot. Curiously oblique, darkly introspective, his words had none of the plangent rhetoric of William Faulkner's 1950 acceptance speech:

Members of the Swedish Academy, ladies and gentlemen. Having no facility for speech-making and no command of oratory, nor any domination of rhetoric, I wish to thank the administrators of the generosity of Alfred Nobel for this prize. No writer who knows the great writers who did not receive the prize can accept it other than with humility. There is no need to list these writers. Everyone here may make his own list according to his knowledge and his conscience. It would be impossible for me to ask the Ambassador of my country to read a speech in which a writer said all of the things which are in his heart. Things may not be immediately discernible in what a man writes and in this, sometimes, he is fortunate, but eventually they are quite clear and by these, and a degree of alchemy that he possesses, he will endure or be forgotten. Writing at its best is a lonely life. Organizations for writers palliate the writer's loneliness but I doubt if they improve his writing. He grows in public stature as he sheds his loneliness and often his work deteriorates. For he does his work alone, and if he is a good enough writer, he must face eternity or the lack of it each day. For a true writer, each book should be a new beginning where he tries again for something that is beyond attainment. He should always try for something that has never been done or that others have tried and failed. Then sometimes, with great luck, he will succeed. How simple the writing of literature would be if it were only necessary to write in another way what has been well written. It is because we have had such great writers in the past that a writer is driven far out past where he can go, out to where no one can help him. I have spoken too long for a writer. A writer should write what he has to say and not speak it. Again I thank you.

In addition to his medal, he received an illuminated scroll and $36,000 in cash. He said the money would come in handy since he owed $8,000. He gave the medal to Mary to keep for a while in her jewelry drawer. Then he gave the medal to the Virgen de Cobre, Cuba's national saint.

The prize had been a long time coming, even though Hemingway's work "was true from the beginning." Why then did the "official" recognition come so belatedly? Reconciling the works of prize winners with the idealistic wishes of Alfred Nobel has posed special problems for the Academy. Nobel had been an admirer of Shelley and had written poems in his style. In 1902 the lofty idealism of such a towering world figure as Ibsen had not been recognized by the Academy, which rejected him as "the bleak champion of negativity." That Hemingway, the author of *nada*, got it and Ibsen had not, is a measure both of the Academy's maturing perception and of the changes that the word idealism—no longer connoting edifying and uplifting —has undergone in more than half a century. During the ceremony of Hemingway's award Dr. Ekeberg, the Lord High Chamberlain and president of the Nobel Foundation, said that he thought that Nobel would have approved a freer interpretation of his wishes if he had lived to experience twentieth-century reality and seen its impact upon the minds of contemporary writers.

The award honored the right man for the right reason, but late, and for the wrong book. The occasion of the award had to be *The Old Man* because it was the only worthy and recent work, but disproportionate emphasis upon it as his crowning achievement unjustly subordinates the earlier and greater work to the level of apprentice effort. As a lyric but atavistic retreat from twentieth-century complexity into simplicity and primitivism, *The Old Man* is neither relevant nor representative of that enormous talent which single-handedly made a revolution in the American language. By the end of the twenties, and certainly by 1940 with *For Whom the Bell Tolls*, Hemingway's major contribution had been made. It is to this early work that we look to find the "powerful style-forming mastery."

The rest of this chapter identifies the ideal strain in Hemingway and explains in particular two major, universal qualities which earned him this top international prize: the code and the style. Both are ideal tendencies nourished by a serious and lively concern for values. These ideal tendencies had been there in his work since 1924 with publication of *In Our Time*, either juxtaposed with or under the surface of the "brutal, callous, and cynical signs." The post-war revaluation of Hemingway had made it possible to discern how his work, even the earliest, was not at variance with, but met the Nobel Prize requirements.

In an elegiac moment on the eve of World War I, Henry James said that his generation had not realized what the years had been making for. But Hemingway with unerring prescience had. The award praised Hemingway for honestly reproducing "the genuine features of the hard countenance of the age": he had told the truth about the twentieth-century human condition. His world, writes Philip Young, "is one in which things do not grow and bear fruit, but explode, break, decompose, or are eaten away. It is saved from total misery by visions of endurance, by what happiness the body can give when it does not hurt, by interludes of love which cannot outlast the furlough and by a pleasure in the landscapes of countries and cafés one can visit. A man has dignity only as he can walk with a courage that has no purpose beyond itself. . . . It is a barren world of fragments which lies before us like a land of bad dreams, where a few pathetic idylls and partial triumphs relieve the otherwise steady diet of nightmare. It has neither light nor love that lasts nor certitude nor peace nor much help for pain. It is swept with the actualities of struggle and flight, and up ahead in the darkness the armies are engaged."

Critics protest this world, arguing that it is too narrow a representation of life, yet the Nobel award praised his verisimilitude. "We do not do badly to protest Hemingway's world," Young continues. "It is not the one we wish to live in, and we usually believe that indeed we do not live in it," but it is a good guess "that while other writers were watching the side acts, Hemingway's eyes have been from the start riveted on the main show. 'Peace in our time' was an obscure and ironic prophecy." His chief distinction within this world is that he told the truth, first about the American experience, then about the European experience, and finally, about the human experience, with such precision and intensity that his stories have become paradigms for the universal experience of everyman in our time.

To tell the truth of this hard countenance and its impact upon people, he had undertaken the demolition of the heritage of the genteel tradition: its bad ideals. They were bad because they were free-floating, perpetuated by received opinion, and led to error because they had no built-in controls. Nowhere were they subjected to the test of reality, the test of one's personal experience. The point of Hemingway's fiction is that ideals and abstractions should never rise on the ladder of abstraction above that level where they can be supported by corroborating evidence. In the self-correcting method of science, ideals and generalizations are subject to the test of experience and can be modified, corrected. Metaphysical truth, on the other hand, could go terribly wrong (consider the slaughter of the Albigenses, the acts justified in the name of the sacred fatherland), because it was not subject to the corrective controls of experience.

The worst kind of idealism for Hemingway was the denial of evil. The doctor in "The Doctor and the Doctor's Wife" is as angry with his wife as with the Indian who has insulted him to get out of repaying him in work for pulling his squaw through pneumonia. "Dear, I don't think, I really don't think that any one would really do a thing of that sort intentionally." Another bad ideal was the social ethic which denied the integrity of individual personality. In "Soldier's

Home," the returned veteran Krebs is cut off by his war experience from his mother's Procrustean, "wholesome" values. His attempt to find the right way for himself conflicts with social orthodoxy:

> "God has some work for every one to do," his mother said. "There can be no idle hands in His Kingdom."
> "I'm not in His Kingdom," Krebs said.
> "We are all of us in His Kingdom." . . .
> "The boys are all settling down; they're all determined to get somewhere; you can see that boys like Charley Simmons are on their way to being really a credit to the community. . . . We want you to enjoy yourself. But you are going to have to settle down to work, Harold. Your father doesn't care what you start in at. All work is honorable as he says. . . ."
> "Is that all?" Krebs said.
> "Yes. Don't you love your mother, dear boy?"
> "No," Krebs said.
> His mother looked at him across the table. Her eyes were shiny. She started crying.
> "I don't love anybody," Krebs said.

Robert Cohn's romantic idealism in *The Sun Also Rises* is a form of received opinion that prevents him from seeing things as they are and this irritates Jake. Cohn considers *The Purple Land* a "sound" book and tells Jake that Brett is "very nice," to which Jake replies bluntly, "She's a drunk." The romantic eye of the naturalist in "A Natural History of the Dead" is not observing the real thing. The test of experience gives the lie with savage sarcasm to conventional affirmations of piety:

> It has always seemed to me that the war has been omitted as a field for the observations of the naturalist. . . . When that persevering traveller, Mungo Park, was at one period

of his course fainting in the vast wilderness of an African
desert, naked and alone . . . a small moss-flower of extraordinary beauty caught his eye. . . . "Can that Being who
planted, watered and brought to perfection, in this obscure
part of the world, a thing which appears of so small importance, look with unconcern upon the situation and suffering of creatures formed after his own image? Surely not.
Reflections like these would not allow me to despair; I
started up and, disregarding both hunger and fatigue,
travelled forward, assured that relief was at hand; and I was
not disappointed."

With a disposition to wonder and adore in like manner . . .
can any branch of Natural History be studied without increasing that faith, love and hope which we also, every one
of us, need in our journey through the wilderness of life?
Let us therefore see what inspiration we may derive from
the dead.

What follows is clinically detailed observation of the
landscape of the dead. It was "amazing that the human
body should be blown into pieces which exploded along no
anatomical lines, but rather divided as capriciously as the
fragmentation in the burst of a high explosive shell. . . .
Until the dead are buried they change somewhat in appearance each day. The color change in Caucasian races is
from white to yellow, to yellow-green, to black. . . . The
dead grow larger each day."

The militant idealism of war rhetoric in which bad ideals
and big abstractions devalue truth is part of the same tradition which insulates human experience with honorific stock
responses instead of illuminating it with concrete diction.
The patriot Gino's remark in *A Farewell to Arms* leads to
Frederick Henry's reflection in which semantic disillusion
gives way to semantic rebirth and belief in the concrete:

"We won't talk about losing. There is enough talk about losing. What has been done this summer cannot have been done in vain."

I did not say anything. I was always embarrassed by the words sacred, glorious, and sacrifice and the expression in vain. We had heard them, sometimes standing in the rain almost out of earshot, so that only the shouted words came through, and had read them, on proclamations that were slapped up by billposters over other proclamations, now for a long time, and I had seen nothing sacred, and the things that were glorious had no glory and the sacrifices were like the stockyards at Chicago if nothing was done with the meat except to bury it. There were many words that you could not stand to hear and finally only the names of places had dignity. Certain numbers were the same way and certain dates and these with the names of the places were all you could say and have them mean anything. Abstract words such as glory, honor, courage, or hallow were obscene beside the concrete names of villages, the numbers of roads, the names of rivers, the numbers of regiments and the dates.

The award asserted a kind of justice in confirming the prophetic manifesto made by the first American to win the prize, Sinclair Lewis, in his Nobel acceptance speech on "The American Fear of Literature," which he had delivered in Stockholm twenty-four years earlier, in 1930. He had more to say than either Faulkner or Hemingway in their acceptance speeches. Dispensing with conventional platitudes, he spoke home truths intended to change America's mode of self-regard: The long-entrenched genteel tradition was the enemy of good, new writing in America. Dreiser's work "had the most benefit to mankind in clearing away the lies and presenting the truth." American writers must resist the strong prescriptive and stultifying forces exerted upon them by patriotic pressure to glorify and prettify American life. Instead, they should write the truth.

By 1954 both of the young Americans whom he had praised for "doing such passionate and authentic work that it makes me sick to see that I am a little too old to be one of them" had received this top international prize: Ernest Hemingway, "educated by the most intense experience, disciplined by his own high standards, an authentic artist whose home is in the whole of life," and William Faulkner, "who has freed the South from hoop-skirts."

Both of these two highly original American Nobel winners were loners, apolitical, who disparaged each other, liked to hunt, seemed glad yet embarrassed at either the Nobel publicity or the public demands it made upon them, and believed in the ideal of human justice, but wrote in radically different styles. While defining between them the formal limits of modern prose fiction, they had wrenched the very warp and woof of American prose fiction into new and rich patterns of possibility for writers to come. The difference between them is the difference between Ciceronean and Attic styles, between the method of extensity in the novel and the method of intensity in the short story. Faulkner's Ciceronean style stresses amplitude. His sentence is loose, complex, and occasionally nonstop, and conventional syntax is abandoned to rely on the rush and thrust of the feeling to sustain the sense. "My ambition is to put everything into one sentence," he told Malcolm Cowley. In impassioned, verbally self-conscious passages, the style soars to an *O altitudo*. In contrast, Hemingway's curt style emphasizes objectivity, highly selective detail, minimal metaphor, and flat, neutral, concrete diction couched most frequently in simple declarative sentences.

The language of their respective Nobel acceptance speeches is instructive. Faulkner's overwrought speech, several cuts above the simple American piney-woods vernacular (Faulkner had told the Swedish reporters, "There is no use pretending. I am not a literary man. I am a farmer that just likes to tell stories.") but perhaps appropriate for the stately European ceremony and aristocratic court whose grace and charm had so moved Yeats in 1923, is ceremonial, rhetorically flushed, grandiloquent, and solemn with the metaphysical strain, and his carefully cadenced seer's utterance aspires to the sublime. Faulkner delivered it in the first evening dress he ever wore. His subject, the human condition. His message, man will not only endure, but prevail. His tone, mantic. Hemingway, safely at Stockholm in proxy, wrote perfunctory remarks on his aesthetic. Whereas Faulkner is deeply involved in what he is making and saying, Hemingway is detached, cool, professional, without enthusiasm. His words are simple, homely, he is far less ambitious, displays a touch of *hubris* in impersonating his last character, Santiago, and is obviously eager to have done. His subject, the writer. His message, it is lonely work, and it may drown one. His tone, terse and guarded conviction.

In fiction their treatment of the same *donnée*, the crucifixion, confirms these stylistic distinctions. Faulkner wrote *A Fable*, an epic, teeming, horizon blue, allegorical novel in which a French corporal reincarnates the Christ and is executed for leading the mutinies which were one of the few redeeming signs of sanity in that iron time. The literal

level of this novel, which Faulkner monitored by posting
status notes and chapter outlines on the walls of his study,
is a detailed account of the war on the western front, and
the novel's extensity perfectly captures the sense of weari-
ness and attrition of trench warfare. For sheer horror,
nausea, and outrage, Faulkner's description of the selection
and removal of the unknown soldier from the underground
depths of Verdun rivals anything in Hemingway, including
his clinically definitive naturalist's vision of the landscape
of the dead. Hemingway, in contrast, wrote a five-page
drama with four characters, "Today Is Friday," in which he
peeled away two millennia of Christian tradition and con-
notation to reveal a human Christ and how he might have
looked historically to the Roman soldiers, one of whom
says to his buddy, "You see me slip the old spear into him?"

Hemingway was deeply international, a citizen of the
world, while Faulkner was provincial. Hemingway was
expatriate, cosmopolitan, a professional traveler, had been
close to Joyce, Eliot, Ford, Fitzgerald, Stein, Pound, and
Sylvia Beach, had studied the bullfight, made safari, liked
strange sights, made the celebrity columns, flew with the
R.A.F., liberated Paris before General Leclerc, liked to
drink, married four times, lived first at Key West—as far
away from the United States as he could and still be in it—
and then in Cuba, and his finest nonliterary moment was his
contribution to the Spanish Loyalist cause, which was to
become the Allied cause in World War II. Faulkner, on the
other hand, was quiet, unassuming, liked to drink, retired
early after a stint of wartime flying to the family home in
Oxford, and sank his roots into the Mississippi mud, culti-
vating his garden, Yoknapatawpha County, and wrote
prodigiously. He was not hung up by the wars as Heming-

way had been, and so he was freer to deal with a wider range of themes and more complex social problems.

His big theme is outrage at white injustice to the Negro, at what Swedish sociologist Gunnar Myrdal called an American dilemma. Since this theme necessarily draws Faulkner into the southern past and the analysis of guilt, his Ciceronean technique evolves complex time dimensions to suggest how present character is determined by, expressive of, and suffers for past injustices. He affirms Negro dignity and humanity and the brotherhood of man, the ideal dearest to Nobel, and perhaps he is doing it more seriously, concretely, and convincingly, where it matters most, in the American South, than Hemingway does with Robert Jordan's somewhat vague convictions, echoing John Donne's sermon, about why he fights in the Spanish Civil War.

The reason, perhaps, is that Hemingway, locked into his own myth and anxiety of the self, looks into the lonely, alienated self (Nelson Algren has called his theme "the affliction of isolation") rather than to society with its complex, shifting human relationships, and, like the ancient mariner, tells essentially the same story—permutations of his own most deeply felt experience projected and transformed into fictional characters. He creates no gigantic mythical world populated with dozens of characters, such as the Snopes, in the Dickensian manner. In his timeless universe of the immediate now, character is illuminated rather than developed. Faulkner's subject is the American South, Hemingway's is himself. Every book of Faulkner's is a new attempt with stylistic innovations. He grew, developed, changed, while Hemingway so intensified his theme that out of the self he made everyman in our time.

The measure of Hemingway's success was Attic: how much could he throw away? The measure of Faulkner's success, Ciceronean: how much could he retain of an enormous verbal richness? But Hemingway did one thing consummately—better than Faulkner or anyone else—he renovated the American language by writing in a new style which made it much more difficult to lie. His own comment was that he had contributed to American literature "a certain clarification of the language which is now in the public domain." This admirable language was applied to the problem of conduct to develop the code, the first of our two major ideals.

Even the concession of the Academy that Hemingway's earlier work was "at variance with the Nobel Prize requirements for a work of ideal tendencies" visited a peculiarly quixotic judgment upon Hemingway. From the very beginning, as Delmore Schwartz showed in 1938, Hemingway's work had expressed a deep moral concern which could not have better met Alfred Nobel's specifications. This was the problem of conduct which Hemingway was to resolve in developing the code. Nobel had hoped that human conduct could be reformed either by making weapons so lethal that men in their rationality would recoil from using them or by forming pacificist organizations. But Hemingway believed that any reform (he would never have used the word) if it was to be achieved, must begin with the reform of the individual and be self-willed and self-generated, not legislated from without by an abstract authority.

"The Hemingway hero," as James Colvert shows, who "sets out in a world dangerously uncertain in its morality, terrifying in its hostility potential . . . is dedicated to the search for values in the life of action." Like Hemingway, the hero has rejected the traditional nineteenth-century values which have been broken down by scientific discovery and attitude, as well as by the disillusioning experience of a generation in the trenches.

Hemingway's first two major characters, Frederick Henry in *A Farewell to Arms* and Jake Barnes in *The Sun Also Rises*, as well as minor characters such as Krebs, "rebel against a society which relies upon traditional moral attitudes and beliefs no longer expressive of its real nature. The Hemingway hero rejects the reality of conventional values because he can discover in them no relevancy to moral realities, and the ramification of his rejection encompasses not only the traditional attitudes toward values, but the very principle underlying them. This traditional approach to value is based upon the unquestioned assumption that sound value judgments can be made through the abstract formulations of conventional moralizing. Values are determined as absolutes and are conceived as metaphysical realities apart from any relation of the physical world apprehensible to the senses."

Although written after *The Sun Also Rises*, *A Farewell to Arms* comes first in the chronological development and complication of the hero. In Henry's reflection on the irrelevance of the sacred abstractions, we see the rebellion first developing as an intellectual apprehension of a radical discontinuity between the official words and his own experience. After his encounter with the brutal battle police who shoot their own troops in the name of the sacred fatherland and his escape into the Tagliamento River, he emerges reborn—in attitude, which is the purpose of all rebirths—to make his

174

separate peace and go for love and food and drink and Switzerland. Emotionally, this one man's mutiny has a latent pacifism that might have appealed to Nobel's moral sense if not to his commercial judgment, but Hemingway does not deal with the pacifist attitude seriously, in intellectual terms, as he would have had he put Henry in the American Army, or as Faulkner does in the real mutiny within the French Army in *A Fable*; after all, as Catherine says, it is only the Italian Army. But the novel proves happiness after the "separate peace" to be an illusory spasm, and at the end, among the garbage cans and the rain, Frederick Henry is a broken man wounded both physically and emotionally. But he is alive, as many of his Italian friends are not, and he has assumed responsibility in searching for and choosing the values himself.

We see the regeneration and partial postwar recovery from alienation of this man in the figure of Jake Barnes in *The Sun Also Rises*. His war injury has taken considerable from him, but not his manhood. Deeply troubled and tormented by Brett's loveliness, unable to sleep at night without a light, he searches for value in the postwar life of France and Spain. Jake analyzes the values in his conversation with Count Mippipopolous, who bares the white, raised scars of his Abyssinian arrow wounds for Jake and Brett's inspection and says, "It is because I have lived very much that now I can enjoy everything so well. . . . That is the secret. You must get to know the values." During his troubled, sleepless night (reminiscent of Fitzgerald's description in *The Crack-Up* of what it feels like to wake up at three o'clock in the morning), Jake reflects, "You paid some ways for everything that was any good. I paid my way into enough things that I liked, so that I had a good time. . . . I did not care what it was all about. All I wanted to know was how to live in it."

Contrasting with Jake and the problem of conduct are what the indefatigable Carlos Baker calls the "messy" characters, such as Cohn and Mike who are concerned with self-gratification, not value. Cohn is obsessed with sexual conquest and aggressive self-assertion, judges the quality of a bar by the number of bottles, and sleeps on the way to Pamplona instead of seeing the splendid country. Jake is concerned with self-mastery and achieves a little in practicing irony, a mode of self-regard apparent not only early in the novel but in his final conversation with Brett: "Oh, Jake," Brett said, "we could have had such a damned good time together." . . . "Yes," I said. "Isn't it pretty to think so?" Throughout the novel there has been small talk about pity and irony. The point is that Jake has learned the protective advantages of irony over the debilitating effects of self-pity. In this swarming wasteland, shadowed by the epigraph from the preacher of Ecclesiastes and dominated by characters seen close up, the matador Pedro Romero has performed in the middle distance, demonstrating purity of heart and line, and set a standard of conduct based on the code. In fact, a fair index of value is the attitude of the central characters toward the bullfight (Jake in particular, with his informal brotherhood of *aficionados* and Montoya's spiritual examination), which adds up, not to the parody of the brotherhood of the code in the mystical Order of Brusadelli in *Across the River*, but to a solid fraternity of professional craftsmanship based on real knowledge.

Concern for conduct, then, an antipathy to received opinion, and the search for value in the life of action are not just ideal tendencies, but major ideal themes central to Hemingway's two earliest and best novels, both written before 1930.

Conduct is regulated by the code, the most prominent ideal in Hemingway's fiction. It was undoubtedly the code that the Academy was thinking of when it praised his "heroic pathos" and fighting the good fight. The code is a great original organizing pattern of characterization that gives an underlying unity and coherence to Hemingway's work. The code, sometimes called grace under pressure, is an ideal set of beliefs and attitudes, essentially a mode of self-regard, which enables the hero to function in a hostile, destructive world, and if not to prevail, at least to come through with honor and some dignity. The code is seldom stated explicitly in the fiction. Instead, Hemingway's characters demonstrate a characteristic behavior in crisis or pain which Philip Young has explained as a response to a traumatic wound, such as Hemingway himself got at Fossalta and used as a major theme in most of his stories, until its literary exorcism by Colonel Cantwell who returns in *Across the River* to the precise site where he was wounded thirty-two years earlier and erects a highly personal monument. The code is the form of courage conquering fear. Its key is maintaining the correct attitude in adversity, holding tight against pain as is required of the lieutenant of artillery by the inhuman doctor who threw a saucer of iodine into his eyes in "A Natural History of the Dead." The essence of the code is contained in Santiago's rumination, "Man is not made for defeat. A man can be destroyed, but not defeated."

This may sound rather ambitious, but Hemingway is saying that the inner attitude and perfection of the will are more important than circumstance and are what ultimately

177

determine a character and his fate. Mastering the code involves an attitudinal change such as that experienced by Francis Macomber, who sheds fear and learns courage and the inner freedom which follow from the example of Robert Wilson. The white hunter briefly lets down his reserve, for which he is duly embarrassed, to show Macomber his secret sign, a death-defying verbal talisman from Shakespeare: "By my troth, I care not; a man can die but once; we owe God a death and let it go which way it will he that dies this year is quit for the next."

The distinction between the code hero, Wilson, and the Hemingway hero, Macomber, is an important distinction emphasized by Young. Moral perspective is lost if the distinction is ignored and the two kinds of characters confused. Moral perspective contrasts two kinds of behavior, as in "The Gambler, the Nun, and the Radio." The honor of Cayetano, the primitive Mexican gambler who refuses to name his assailant, contrasts with Mr. Frazer's vague, civilized, principled confusions. Cayetano's silence may not be rational or intelligent or productive or may not help others or even help himself, but at least he stands for something, and in standing for something, his life has meaning. Mr. Frazer's awareness is intensified by the example of code hero Cayetano.

In many other stories the initiation theme is dramatized when the hero, a young man, learns important lessons from an older character, who may be his own father as in "Fathers and Sons." This initiation theme, beginning in "Indian Camp," is one of the finest things in Hemingway. Stressing the value of experience-based knowledge (the kind of education which Melville got in the forecastle of a whaler rather than at Yale or Harvard) and emphasizing education in our time rather than in the past (as in the education of Henry Adams), Hemingway works one of the grand archetypes in world fiction, the education and initiation of the young, which is what the Nick Adams stories are all about. There can be no more important ideal tendency. Significantly, in its concern for the big issues and lofty themes, the Swedish Academy did not name this ideal tendency, which makes "Fathers and Sons," with its contrast of three American generations, as worthy a story as *The Old Man* because of the universality of its tender, intensively rendered experience that requires knowledge of all the other stories to bring it to full performance.

Although the lineage of code heroes extends far back into the earliest Nick Adams stories, it is more instructive to see the making of the code rather than to see it perfected in Santiago, or to see behind the code and the expense of spirit in maintaining it in *Across the River*. The damaged Italian major of "In Another Country" represents all Hemingway's code heroes concerned with perfecting the will. Nick Adams, the generic young man of the early stories, tells this one as a volunteer in the Italian Army. The scene is a hospital in Milan in the late years of the war. "In the fall the war was always there, but we did not go to it any more." Nick and four other wounded young men, one with a black handkerchief shielding his shattered face, are taking treatment. Nick's wounded leg is being exercised on one of the new therapy machines. The subject of the story is the major "who had a little hand like a baby's" which is held between two leather straps that bounce up and down and flap the stiff fingers. Before the war, he had been the greatest fencer in Italy. He comes regularly every day for his treatment although he does not believe in the machines.

The point of the story is his behavior and its implicit impact upon young Nick, who is close to him and learning Italian grammar from him.

One day for no apparent reason the major shows intense anger. He condemns the machines as nonsense, "a theory, like another." He calls Nick a "stupid impossible disgrace" because he has not learned his grammar, and speaks very angrily, and bitterly tells Nick that he should not marry because "He'll lose it." "He was looking at the wall. Then he looked down at the machine and jerked his little hand out from between the straps and slapped it hard against his thigh. 'He'll lose it,' he almost shouted. 'Don't argue with me!' Then he called to the attendant who ran the machines. 'Come and turn this damned thing off.'"

The reason for his outburst: his wife has just died of pneumonia. He had not married her until he was definitely invalided out of the war. "He stood there biting his lower lip. 'It is very difficult,' he said. 'I cannot resign myself.' He looked straight past me and out through the window. Then he began to cry. 'I am utterly unable to resign myself,' he said and choked." After three days, the major returned "at the usual hour, wearing a black band on the sleeve of his uniform." The photographs of restored hands which the doctor had hung on the wall in front of the major's machine "did not make much difference to the major because he only looked out of the window."

The story is about the soul *in extremis*. Like Frederick Henry, the major has suffered a double loss, physical and psychological. He has lost everything of value but his life. Like Samson Agonistes, the major is being tested in an ordeal and his will perfected. The title is about the country of the major's mind where discipline wrestles with grief, a country very different from that of Nick's experience. Age, experience, and suffering separate the major, as code hero, from Nick Adams, the Hemingway hero. A different kind of bravery from that which has become commonplace in the trenches is required for him to accept his wife's death. He does not believe in the machine. Yet he carries on, without hope, all passion spent. He demonstrates qualities which distinguish all the code heroes. Having a kind of ultimate knowledge based on his war experience, he is justifiably skeptical of the optimistic expectations of the doctors. His wound and the death of his wife give him a new and painful knowledge. Skilled, a former fencer, he reverts to the discipline of grammar as a way of ordering his responses. His courage is both physical and spiritual as he relies upon himself. He is honest, refusing to accept either the cheery hopes of the doctors or of faith: "I cannot resign myself." He has the integrity of personal discipline. As he once had learned the discipline of grammar and of fencing, now he is achieving a spiritual discipline in maintaining control. Finally, in the bleak scene where, submitting to the machine in which he does not believe, he exercises choice, ignores the photographs installed for his benefit, and looks stoically out the window. In his brief glimpse into another country, Nick has had a lesson in how to behave. In seeing how the code is formed, he has the advantage of more knowledge than Manolin, Santiago's apprentice, who sees only the splendid achievement of Santiago's perfected code in action. Seeing the effort expended to hold tight, Nick knows the cost of the code, whereas Manolin can only infer its cost.

Out of his code comes the style, the second major ideal we are considering. The highest and most specialized form of the code for Hemingway is aesthetic discipline. The same values which maintain the code—knowledge, skill, and integrity—also inform the aesthetic, which is important because it shapes style, and style perpetuates all other values. Style, which integrates all other fictional elements, is his ultimate term, more important even, as his final years show, than life itself. It is his style more than any other achievement that won him the Nobel Prize. A man is what he does, whether he be matador, fisherman, general, prize fighter, doctor, or writer. If he is a writer, how he writes is the most important thing in life. If he forgets this and wastes his talent, he goes bad as did Harry, the writer without discipline, the one with fat on his soul in "The Snows of Kilimanjaro." He jeopardizes his soul. But if he writes well, he may save his soul, attain the icy summit where his work is preserved, and achieve immortality before his time runs out. "The great thing is to last and get your work done and see and hear and learn and understand; and write when there is something that you know. . . . Let those who want to save the world if you can get to see it clear and as a whole. Then any part you make will represent the whole if it's made truly."

Hemingway on the aesthetic is Platonic, whether in parable ("The Snows of Kilimanjaro"), allegory (*The Old Man*), or rumination (*The Green Hills of Africa*). "A country, finally, erodes and the dust blows away, the people all die and none of them were of any importance permanently, except those who practiced the arts. . . . A thousand years makes economics silly and a work of art endures forever, but it is very difficult to do." His ultimate aspiration is to achieve immortality by writing true and worthy books. "A writer ought always to write . . . as if he were going to die at the end of the book." In other words, he should give his all like the bullfighters. "Nobody ever lives their life all the way up except bull-fighters." For Hemingway the bull-fighter is the figure of the artist, and the discipline of art is a form of the code.

The appeal of the bullfight to Hemingway was primarily aesthetic. The matador was above all a stylist and the greatest demonstrated "a purity of line." Writer and mata-dor also have much in common, for both are artists. "Bull-fighting," writes Hemingway, "is the only art in which the artist is in danger of death and in which the degree of brilliance in the performance is left to the fighter's honor." Both are lonely crafts which cannot be taught and demand rare talent, long apprenticeship, and discipline. Both de-mand a style based upon standards and integrity. Shave the horns or write poorly and you deprive your life of its mean-ing. Both are very risky and ruthless. Both culminate in public performance and judgment. The price of failure is extreme: for the matador, destruction of the body; for the writer, the soul.

He went to the bullfights to learn how to write truly, even though he was already an accomplished journalist and foreign correspondent and had served his apprenticeship on the Kansas City *Star* and the Toronto *Star*. In *Death in the Afternoon*, that "Baedeker of bulls," he explains:

> I was trying to write then and I found the greatest diffi-culty, aside from knowing truly what you really felt, rather than what you were supposed to feel, and had been taught to feel, was to put down what really happened in action; what the actual things were which produced the emotion that you experienced. . . . but the real thing, the sequence of motion and fact which made the emotion and which would be as valid in a year or in ten years or, with luck and

if you stated it purely enough, always, was beyond me and I was working very hard to try to get it. The only place where you could see life and death, *i.e.*, violent death now that the wars were over, was in the bull ring and I wanted very much to go to Spain where I could study it. I was trying to learn to write, commencing with the simplest things, and one of the simplest things of all and the most fundamental is violent death. . . . I had read many books in which, when the author tried to convey it, he only produced a blur, and I decided that this was because either the author had never seen it clearly or at the moment of it, he had physically or mentally shut his eyes . . . .

This very important passage summarizes Hemingway's aesthetic. Key elements are truth, individualism, experience, and its validation by one's own witness.

First, the truth. A strenuous honesty is directed toward establishing the truth of what one really felt. A spiritual self-examination is under way. It is as important for the writer as it was for Jake Barnes and Krebs. To this concern for personal truth Hemingway brought a scrupulous honesty and integrity. Once he had started as writer, he refused to compromise his style. Living in Paris, short of money, with wife and child, he accumulated a year's rejection slips, yet refused a lucrative Hearst offer so that he could continue writing as he intended. Fiercely independent, he was always his own man. "Toward his craft," John Peale Bishop comments, "he was humble, and had, moreover, the most complete literary integrity it has ever been my lot to encounter. I say the most complete, for while I have known others who were not to be corrupted, none of them was presented with the opportunities for corruption that assailed Hemingway."

184

Second, this independence stresses a characteristically American self-reliance. This individualism expresses a typically Protestant concern for the individual conscience regardless of public opinion:

> If you serve time for society, democracy, and the other things quite young, and declining any further enlistment make yourself responsible only to yourself, you exchange the pleasant, comforting stench of comrades for something you can never feel in any other way than by yourself. That something I cannot yet define completely but the feeling comes when you write well and truly of something and know impersonally you have written in that way and those who are paid to read it and report on it do not like the subject so they say it is all a fake, yet you know its value absolutely.

Third, the concern for the real thing—experience, not abstractions about experience, full of judgment. His concern is for communicating experience itself in all its dramatic immediacy and concreteness by rediscovering the objective correlative which had produced the experience. And the real thing is to be expressed in a purified language. If experience is stated purely enough with skill comparable to Romero's "purity of line," the result will "be as valid in a year or in ten years or, with luck, and if you stated it purely enough, always."

Honoring experience means rejecting received opinion and the terms of the genteel tradition. Hemingway refuses to accept the "blur," in short, the verbal convention of other writers who had not seen clearly. To write honestly, one must validate what happened by the witness of his own experience up front. When driving, he always liked to sit up front, watching the road and terrain closely as Colonel

Cantwell does. All Hemingway's life was really a search, up front, to see how it truly was in his principal subject, the wars of our time. The weather, the wars, the land—all must be personally witnessed and verified. Writing begins with observation:

> If a writer stops observing he is finished. But he does not have to observe consciously nor think how it will be useful. Perhaps that would be true at the beginning. But later everything he sees goes into the great reserve of things he knows or has seen. If it is any use to know it, I always try to write on the principle of the iceberg. There is seven eighths of it under water for every part that shows. Anything you know you can eliminate and it only strengthens your iceberg. It is the part that doesn't show. If a writer omits something because he does not know it then there is a hole in the story.

This aesthetic ideal, comprised of concern for truth by a self-reliant individual who subjects actual experience to eyewitness examination, informs the act of writing by emerging as a style. Experience-based knowledge in the service of a rigorous discipline enabled Hemingway to achieve in prose an unparalleled verbal economy usually found only in poetry, summarized by the architectural design principle "less is more." The "less" is fewer words, the visible tip of the iceberg, the technical means. The "more" is the surprisingly disproportionate effect. His aim was to strip away all superflux until what remained was like a clean white bone. "I have tried to eliminate everything unnecessary to conveying experience to the reader so that after he or she has read something it will become a part of his or her experience and seem actually to have happened." Story after story—"Indian Camp," "Fathers and Sons," "A

Clean, Well-Lighted Place"—deceptively simple in their terse, realistic surfaces ("Brett's glass was empty.") have this quality of submerged meanings dominating the story. Their effect is an intensity which no other writer has achieved. The older one gets, the more meaning appears, and what one had thought was familiar turns out to be astonishingly fresh and new.

Key features of this style are objectivity, largely what an observer would see or observe if he was to witness the scene; dramatic emphasis employing a terse dialogue; and terse sentences with little subordination. Metaphor is exploited very sparingly, but with absolute precision. Paco, paying for his deadly illusions in "Capital of the World," feels "his life go out of him as dirty water empties from a bathtub when the plug is drawn." We can see these features in the austere, minimal style of "Today Is Friday," a brief play which makes *The Old Man* seem prolix by comparison.

"Today Is Friday" dramatizes the crucifixion as told entirely in dialog by three Roman soldiers who are "a little cock-eyed" drinking in a wineshop after having participated in the crucifixion. "You tried the red?" asks the first soldier, but the third soldier "can't drink the damn stuff. It makes my gut sour." Golgotha has got to him and somatically his gut has got experience-based knowledge that has not yet reached his brain. The Hebrew wine seller fixes him something for his stomach:

3d Soldier—Hey, what you put in that, camel chips?
Wine-seller—You drink that right down, Lootenant. That'll
      fix you up right. . . .
    (*The third Roman soldier drinks the cup down.*)
3d Roman Soldier—Jesus Christ. (*He makes a face.*)
2d Soldier—That false alarm!

1st Soldier—Oh, I don't know. He was pretty good in there
　　　today.

In the praise of the first soldier, Christ has become the
code hero and Golgotha has become all the bad places
where the code hero has suffered and been stigmatized:
Fossalta, the bullring, the prize ring, the trenches, the dark
night of the soul in "A Clean Well-Lighted Place." The
understated but insistently repeated praise of the first
soldier might seem like the last thing that should be said
about Christ, but in the context of Hemingway's work and
values, it becomes peculiarly appropriate. Here is an instructive case of apparent "cynical and callous signs" which
actually shows an important "ideal tendency." In this play
Hemingway as writer sets himself an enormously difficult
aesthetic challenge requiring an objectivity almost impossible to achieve. Deflate the Christ story of metaphysical
received opinion and empirically, skeptically subject what
must have been his experience to the test of one's own personal experience and see what remains. A whole new
dimension of Christ, Hemingway's dimension, is revealed:
the historical Christ as code hero in whose shadow walks
every admirable figure in Hemingway.

Twenty centuries of Christianity and its tradition are
stripped away to discover how it might actually have appeared to the men of the time. Christian spirituality has
evaporated—no halo, no resurrection, no spiritual apotheo-
sis, only just another tough case. Deliberately and without
eloquence, Hemingway reveals Christ as code hero without
benefit of eternity and Christian immortality. He has replaced a large ideal with a limited one. He uses dramatic
irony to achieve an enormous concentration and intensity

within this tight, reductive limitation before history. Unlike the characters, we view the story's events through the distorting perspective of two millenia of the tradition. Inevitably for us, but not the soldiers, the red wine lies beyond metaphor, symbolizing the sacrament. Again, as in his manual of the bullfight, Hemingway has rejected received opinion and in an audacious leap of the realistic imagination worked his way back in time to how it might have been on that first Good Friday. In contrasting this play with just one of the many conventions of rendering the crucifixion, painting, for example, it becomes apparent how original Hemingway's treatment is, and how different in its brevity from Faulkner's extended, allegorical *A Fable*.

Although subdued and occasional allusions in *The Old Man* suggest Santiago as a Christ figure, the most striking difference between "Today Is Friday" and *The Old Man* is stylistic. The canon of economy has been abandoned, and extensity replaces intensity. *The Old Man* is actually an expanded anecdote, which contains two prolix elements, cetology and Santiago's expansive ruminations. Neither element appears in Hemingway's earlier fiction. In his "Cetology" chapter and elsewhere in *Moby Dick*, Melville described at length in documentary style the lore of whaling and the technology of the fishery. Similarly, Hemingway prolongs the old man's story by describing in detail the ocean scene and the process of fishing. What he once wrote of Melville applies to *The Old Man*: "We have had writers of rhetoric who had the good fortune to find a little, in a chronicle of another man and from voyaging, of how things, actual things, can be, whales for instance, and this knowledge is wrapped in the rhetoric like plums in a pudding." Additional extensity consists of Santiago's ruminations. Unlike such early stories as "Big Two-Hearted River," in which we infer states of minds and emotions by the objectively rendered scene with an absolute minimum of being told explicitly what the characters are thinking, in *The Old Man* we are shown the contents of Santiago's mind: affection and hero worship for DiMaggio; dreams of lions on the African beaches; musings about killing the stars; and the boy. We are even shown what is in Hemingway's mind and could never be enunciated by Santiago in the terms attributed to him: "A man can be destroyed, but not defeated." The point is stated didactically in terms reminiscent of and more appropriate to Faulkner's acceptance speech than to the simple Santiago. Here the literary moral is stated, as it seldom is in the early stories where the meaning is larger than the means. But *The Old Man* is larger and longer than its meaning. It is a matter of proportion and scale.

Through the expanded rhetoric and pastoral simplification of his final style, Hemingway seeks to make the romantic ideal of heroic pathos credible. The story is credible as primitive ritual in which Santiago as hunter exemplifies the tribal values necessary for survival in Plato's cave when life was nasty, brutish, and short. But *The Old Man* is not a tale for our time. Now that supermarkets have replaced the hunt in our civilized and crowded time, the values we need are intelligence more than knowledge, prudence and restraint more than action and excess, *communitas* more than the affliction of isolation, compassion more than rapacity—the very values of authentic human brotherhood which Alfred Nobel had cherished and which Hemingway celebrated in Zurito, Robert Jordan, Anselmo, the lieutenant of artillery, and the older waiter in "A Clean Well-Lighted

Place." Today we desperately need the courage of intelligence, not romantic myths of individual self-reliance on the frontier. The courage of the open boat or men against the sea or nature or space, although diverting, like professional football, is not of the highest relevance for our particular and immediate crisis. If we honored the courage of intelligence as we do the courage of the code, we might not have to hold so tight.

Just as code heroes Manuel and Santiago obsessively keep fighting and fishing, so Hemingway keeps writing, going out too far. In his acceptance speech alluding to Santiago— "Beyond all people in the world"—Hemingway says that because of the great writers of the past, "a writer is driven far out past where he can go, out to where no one can help him." In *The Old Man* he has written an allegory of the writer wrestling with his art. Now in his mind, life and art become transposed. As the driven writer, he is the old man, and the act of writing is actually the heroic pathos cited in the award. Instead of being the driven writer, he could have been creative in more comfortable ways, but he has become a prisoner of his own code and of his own gigantic, unreasonable ideal of what constituted achievement for him, Ernest Hemingway: to defend his title against all comers. He is governed by his own rigid mode of self-regard, that of the champion who "beat Mr. Turgenev . . . beat Mr. de Maupassant . . . fought two draws with Mr. Stendhal," not who and what he is.

Hemingway once correctly described his contribution to American literature as "a certain clarification of the language which is now in the public domain." This would have been enough for many writers, but it was not for a writer of Hemingway's ambitions and ego, *i.e.*, ideals. He could not quit when he was ahead. He had to keep forging ahead even if he were not. Rising at first light to write, he was in the iron service of a lifetime discipline which would not let go. He was pursuing inhuman, romantic ultimates out of Keats (the demon-ideal of art), Browning (the reach should exceed the grasp), and Tennyson ("To strive, to seek, to find, and not to yield"). A prisoner of his own abstractions—those which in his expatriate youth he had so painstakingly forged out of the materials of the bullfight to replace the hypocritical sacred terms of the genteel tradition—he was doomed to go through the habitual motions, learned over a lifetime, even if all he could produce was "The Dangerous Summer" or the bittersweet *A Moveable Feast*, with its nostalgia for his youth in Paris. This effort has its admirable aspect. "As I saw it," wrote Lillian Ross, "he was heroically and uncorruptedly and uncompromisingly occupied day after day with writing as hard as *he could* and as well as *he could* until the day he died." Nevertheless, the first decade of his writing life had been intensely productive; the second, less; and the last two, barren. He had no new material, no new ground to cover. He was reduced to recycling his past.

JOHN STEINBECK

by Warren G. French

After the nobel prize for Literature had been bestowed—most critics agreed deservedly—upon Faulkner
and Hemingway, speculation arose about the next American winner. Sentiment in the United States favored the
venerable Robert Frost, who had been regarded for nearly
half a century as the nation's most representative poetic
voice. His colloquial language and Yankee philosophy, however, seem to have been too intimately associated with New
England to be fully appreciated by Europeans, who did not
share the region's laconic Puritanical pragmatism.

Certainly John Steinbeck's name played only a small part
in Nobel Prize speculations. If the amount of critical writing about an author is any index of his reputation, Faulkner's dismissal of Steinbeck as a "journalist" reflected a
general sentiment.[1] Yet in November, 1962, it was an-

---

[1] "Steinbeck is just a reporter, a newspaperman, not really a writer."
(*Faulkner at Nagano*, ed. by Robert A. Jelliffe [Tokyo, 1956], 7.) During
the year that Steinbeck received the Nobel Prize, he was—according to the
MLA bibliography—the subject of one short book and three related articles;
whereas, four books and seventy other pieces of work about Faulkner and
six books and thirty-three other writings about Hemingway appeared.

nounced to the surprise of everyone, including—if we can believe newspaper reports—the author himself, that Steinbeck had been selected.

Steinbeck himself in a letter to the *Colorado Quarterly* described criticism as "a kind of ill tempered parlour game in which nobody gets kissed." He might have been describing the reaction to the announcement of his selection for the Nobel Prize—the little that there was. The lack of anything approaching a national literary newspaper is brought home sharply to one seeking reports of the immediate response to items of literary news.

We have, of course, God's plenty of quarterlies; but most deliberately pride themselves on existing outside the accidents of time, promoting their own discoveries and grinding private axes. The *Saturday Review*, once of "Literature," had become so involved by 1962 with records, travel, education, the mass media, and anything else that it hoped might attract someone's attention that it could not even find room to note that an American author had received the international literary prize.

The announcement provoked nationally circulated comment only in such weekly chronicles as *Time* and *Newsweek*, the former of which unleashed an especially vicious anonymous attack, claiming that "critics" (none identified by name) disapproved the award and calling *The Grapes of Wrath* a "limited" work of fiction, "scarcely able to survive its time and place." The *New Republic* offered little more comfort with an observation that "three of the six Nobel awards to Americans have gone to writers who, far from being nationally esteemed among the finest of their time, are not even considered first-rate." An editorial writer for the *New York Times* was more temperate and grateful to the Committee for recognizing American talent, yet even he observed that "the international character of the award and the weight attached to it raise questions about the mechanics of selection and how close the Nobel committee is to the main currents of American writing."

Sophisticated reaction to the award is best and most permanently summed up in an article prepared for the *New York Times Book Review* (December 9, 1962) by Arthur Mizener, Scott Fitzgerald's biographer, apparently the only piece by a major American critic especially commissioned to meditate upon the award and adjudge its appropriateness. The opening sentence crystallized the condescending tone of most reactions: "Probably everyone who was adult in the late thirties has a special warm spot in his memory for the books John Steinbeck wrote then."

Mizener went on to observe that the response "we" felt then to *In Dubious Battle* and *The Grapes of Wrath* "seemed to be wholly justified by Steinbeck's lesser works of the period, in which his strong sympathy for the poor and simple and his deep if sentimental conviction of their purity of heart were displayed in happy, charming books like *Tortilla Flat* (1935) and in tragedies of the joys and sufferings of the young—whether in fact or in mental development—such as *The Red Pony* (1936) and *Of Mice and Men* (1937)." After *The Grapes of Wrath*, however, Mizener continued, "most serious readers seem to have ceased to read him." He found it "a fascinating if somewhat melancholy task to reread these books in the sixties when our feelings are no longer under the special influences that affected them strongly in the thirties."

The attitudes that Mizener articulated were challenged only much later in the specialized journal *Books Abroad,*

in which Alba della Fazia said that Steinbeck and the previous year's winner, Yugoslav Ivo Andrič, were "qualified
recipients," who "achieve coincidence in their sympathy for
idealism and their antipathy to oppression." Steinbeck
seems indeed a prophet without honor in his own country,
except among ordinary readers who have bought his novels
for years in both original and paperback editions.

Such popularity with the *hoi polloi* is in itself, of course,
enough to make one suspect among American critics. The
propounder of what has remained "authorized opinion"
about Steinbeck is Edmund Wilson, who some enthusiasts
thought should have received the Nobel award in Steinbeck's place. In *The Boys in the Back Room*, a study of
California writers originally published in the *New Republic*
in 1940, just after the appearance of *The Grapes of Wrath*,
Wilson made it known that "the chief subject of Mr. Steinbeck's fiction has been . . . not those aspects of humanity in
which it is most thoughtful, imaginative, constructive, nor
even those aspects of animals that seem most attractive to
humans, but rather the processes of life itself."

In the thirties—as anyone who undertakes the melancholy
task of studying literary and motion picture censorship during the Depression becomes aware—a preoccupation with
the "processes of life itself" was considered almost as im-
proper in New York as in Berlin, Moscow, or Madrid, where
political ideologies provided the justification for suspend-
ing these processes whenever they proved inconvenient to
elitist aspirations. Wilson's statement places him as one of
the most respected defenders of one of the principal de-
terrents to the development of dynamic thought and culture
in the United States, the genteel tradition.

I do not wish to digress here by attempting to define this

tradition or exploring all its stultifying ramifications; but, in order to clarify my approach to Steinbeck's fiction, I must comment on what I feel is a principal tenet underlying this tradition: man is not an organism that has accidentally developed a still quite imperfectly exploited capacity to reason, but an instrument of reason that is accidentally—and lamentably—also a biological organism. Superficial decorum is thus exalted above the dignity of the basic life processes themselves.

Wilson quite rightly suspected that Steinbeck (whose "unpanicky scrutiny of life" the critic grudgingly admired) was in his early, most productive years an unswerving opponent of the cant of those adherents to the genteel tradition who closed the window at polite sherry parties to shut out the smell of Hoovervilles burning in California, the sounds of mass executions in Russia, the sight of concentration camps springing up in the Germany of Kant and Fichte. Steinbeck struck out at those who would shed blood in the name of bloodless abstractions. He used the only weapon at a writer's disposal, scathing criticism. The Wilsons and Mizeners led the group that responded with traditional withering condescension toward those who dared affirm the value of "the processes of life" over political and social abstractions.

The aim of Steinbeck's writing is suggested by one of the few direct answers he gave newsmen barraging him with questions during an interview following the announcement of his Nobel award. Asked "What is the major function of an author in today's society?," he replied, "Criticism, I should think."

The importance of this reply is often missed, I think, because many people take for granted that criticism is the writer's function and find nothing surprising in his saying so. Yet the concept of the creative writer as fundamentally a social critic is distinctly unfashionable today. The mainstream of twentieth-century writing flowing through Joyce, Lawrence, and Hemingway has been focused not upon criticism, which is directed ultimately at social reform, but upon self-realization. The attitude, which is reflected most vividly in the popular writings of J. D. Salinger, is that society is corrupted beyond the possibility of reform and that the only problem the individual can hope to cope with is that of arriving at a satisfactory personal adjustment to a world that he cannot hope to renovate. (Joyce, of course, criticized Ireland, but because it frustrated his characters, not because he wanted to urge specific reforms.) So influential indeed has the literature of self-realization become that even the social criticism that abounds in the novels of a writer like Faulkner has been overlooked during the rush to explicate its psychological and mythical aspects.

Criticism, of course, is never popular. William Golding in "Fable," an essay explaining something of his intentions in *Lord of the Flies*, discusses the fool in *King Lear*:

> though Shakespeare nowhere says so, it is plain enough to me that Lear's daughters got him in the end. For the fool was a fabulist, and fabulists are never popular. They are those people who haunt the fringes of history and appear in miscellanies of anecdotes as slaves or jesters, rash courtiers, or just plain wise men. They tell the dictator, the absolute monarch what he ought to know but does not want to hear. Generally they are hanged, or beheaded or even bowstringed. . . . Why this is so is clear enough. The fabulist is a moralist. He cannot make a story without a human lesson tucked away in it.

Golding's essay reminds us that the fabulist's vehicle must be parable, because if the writer-critic is to make a valid and useful criticism of society, he must create characters who are not individuals in quest of unique identities, but allegorical representatives of mankind as a whole. He must create a convincingly specific situation that mirrors a recognizably general one. If his work is not to degenerate into the manipulation of lifeless counters, he must create figures and environments credible enough to interest and absorb readers in themselves. Few writers succeed in achieving this fusion of the believably individual and the significantly general.

Steinbeck has had quite uneven success in achieving this difficult fusion, but for the ten-year period between 1935 and 1945, he produced results that few other writers have equalled. If his later works, like his earliest, fail to measure up to the standard he set for himself during one period, one may regret his decline, but one is by no means justified in feeling that what had already been accomplished is thereby devalued. Most writers are judged by their successes, not their failures; but Golding explains that the moralist may not always be judged by objective critical standards because he must make "an unforgiveable assumption; namely that he knows better than his reader."

Part of the hypercritical judgment of Steinbeck very likely results, however, from the failure to recognize that he is not essentially a realist or a naturalist or a reporter or a propagandist, but—as essential in order to exercise his self-appointed function as critic—a fabulist. Only when he is regarded as basically a fabulist can his successes be clearly distinguished from his failures and can the consistent concept of art responsible for the creation of both understood.

Furthermore, despite the superficial diversity of his writings, I believe that they are nearly all efforts to treat allegorically the same basic subject—and that the one just likely to affront American defenders of the genteel tradition, the evils of respectability.

Steinbeck's penchant for attacking respectability through fable is unsubtly manifested in his first published novel, *Cup of Gold*, a romantic fantasy about the famous Caribbean pirate, Sir Henry Morgan. This novel, which was received upon publication in 1929 without enthusiasm and soon lapsed into obscurity, would surely have disappeared from sight altogether if it were not for the drawing power later works bestowed upon the author's name. Even a summary of the lurid plot, centering upon a buccaneer's pursuit of a woman of legendary beauty, would serve little purpose today; what matters is that the novel depicts the destruction of an outstanding individual's potential by the forces of respectability.

Early in the novel Merlin, resurrected from the days of King Arthur, tells a young Welsh hillbilly:

> "You want the moon to drink from as a golden cup; and so, it is very likely that you will become a great man—if only you remain a little child. All the world's great have been little boys who wanted the moon; running and climbing, they sometimes caught a firefly. But if one grow to a man's mind, that mind must see that it cannot have the moon and would not want it if it could—and so, it catches no fireflies."

Sure enough, as long as Morgan remains a childlike adventurer, sailing the Spanish Main and sacking cities, he is a great man; but when he falls into the British king's hands and instead of being beheaded is knighted and made lieutenant governor, the apparent elevation leads to the fulfillment of Merlin's darkest prophecy. Morgan loses his self-confidence, confessing as he sentences some former fellow renegades to the gallows, "Civilization will split up a character, and he who refuses to split goes under." Respectability has destroyed the boy in him, so that he catches no more fireflies. At his death, "the fire went out of the embers with a dry, hard snap."

After *Cup of Gold,* the stream of Steinbeck's career meanders into the kind of vast swamp that so long delayed the discovery of the source of the Nile. Although his second published book was *The Pastures of Heaven,* Peter Lisca in *The Wide World of John Steinbeck* offers convincing evidence that this novel was composed after the third to be published, *To a God Unknown.* Certainly the latter provides a more satisfactory link between the romantic fantasy of the first novel and the superficially realistic tales of Steinbeck's major period that begins with *The Pastures of Heaven.*

To a God Unknown is deservedly one of Steinbeck's least admired works. A grotesque, episodic tale that makes sense only if read allegorically, it tells of the way in which Joseph Wayne at last brings rain to a parched California wasteland by making a human sacrifice of himself and his wife. Overabundant symbolism suggests that Steinbeck was tempted early in his career to add to the growing pile of works exploiting the kind of literary patterns made fashionable by T. S. Eliot.

Even in this novel, however, respectability proves the culprit. Along with the droll short story, "Saint Katy the Virgin," *To a God Unknown* appears a relic of a period during which Steinbeck directed his criticism principally against the traditional church as a perpetuator of destructive respectability.

He had shown little love for the church in *Cup of Gold*. When Morgan threatens to sack Panama City, Steinbeck satirizes the Spanish defenders' running to the church rather than to the city walls to protect themselves. In *To a God Unknown* the church is again portrayed as an ineffectual luxury. When Joseph requests a prayer for rain, the parish priest replies, "The principal business of God has to do with men . . . their progress toward heaven, and their punishment in Hell." Joseph rejects this sanctimonious attitude, but fails himself to propound a social gospel that would provide an alternative to the unworldly preoccupations of the traditional church. Just as "the last man in the Western World to see the sun," whom Joseph meets on a trip into the hills, has developed a private religion that enables him to identify himself with the sun, so Joseph attains a lonely identification with the soil that he loves—but only at the cost of his life. As the parish priest observes with a relief bordering on heresy, "Thank God this man has no message. Thank God he has no will to be remembered, to be believed in . . . else there might be a new Christ here in the West."

At the time he was writing this novel, Steinbeck seems to have lost faith in the efficacy of collective social action and to have come to the disillusioned belief of many artists of the "wasteland" period that the world could be saved only by an individual's sacrificial gesture. Joseph Wayne's action stands at the remotest pole from Tom Joad's vision of himself as a symbol of collective humanity in *The Grapes of Wrath*.

Steinbeck abandoned the awkward allegorical form of *To a God Unknown* in his next novels, but he only slowly moved away from Morgan's theory in *Cup of Gold* that those who refuse to "split before civilization must go under. The principal characters in the next four long works do indeed go under.

The Pastures of Heaven has often been treated as a loosely related collection of short stories with a unifying setting, but, as I have argued in my *John Steinbeck*, in each episode some member of a family named Munroe "wreaks havoc by misjudging some aspect of a situation or by thoughtlessly saying or doing the wrong thing." "The Munroes are not only at fault in each episode, but each error is graver than the preceding," so that the stories constitute a carefully unified novel depicting the harm done unintentionally by respectable people seeking only to do "the right thing." Steinbeck pictures this family, whose only quest is to get rich quick and then freeze into an unchanging status, as headed by a father who "by stroke after stroke of genius" makes his house "look like a hundred thousand other country houses in the west" and boasting a son whose "knowledge of the world" results in "a firm intention to give over one's life to science after gutting it of emotional possibilities." The family feels that it is laboring under a curse, and, indeed, everything that comes into contact with the members is blighted. Steinbeck's attitude, however, is that the curse is no manifestation of supernatural malice, but a result of the Munroes' own lack of feeling for the processes of life. They are a baneful influence because they are so entirely attuned to achieving financial success and establishing a status quo that they have lost any sensitivity to the rhythms of life and to the feelings of other people.

The weakness of *The Pastures of Heaven* as a fable is that Steinbeck creates such a profusion of ironies that the central theme often disappears beneath a torrent of details. Although his next novel, *Tortilla Flat*, was also episodic, in it the struggle between material success and natural goodness, symbolized in the career of Danny—one of the *paisanos* of Mexican descent who live in the hills above Monterey, California—clearly emerges as the central theme.

Steinbeck's preface to the novel stresses Danny's closeness to nature: "If the growing Danny preferred to sleep in the forest, to work on ranches, and to wrest his food and wine from an unwilling world, it was not because he did not have influential relatives." However, when Danny inherits two houses after World War I, he is "a little weighed down with the responsibility of ownership." When he goes with a friend to take possession, Pilon notices that the "worry of property was settling on Danny's face. No more in life would that face be free of care. No more would Danny break windows now that he had windows of his own to break."

Pilon's fears are not fully justified. Danny abandons his inheritance and makes a flamboyant attempt to return to his old, wild life, stealing from his own house and friends. Having once succumbed to respectability, however, he cannot meet the rigorous demands of life in the woods. Exhausted upon his return, the Danny "who had fought for lost causes, or any other kind," now "sat on his front porch in the sunlight, his blue-jeaned knees drawn up against his chest, his hands dangling from limp wrists, his head bent forward as though by a heavy black thought. His eyes had no light of desire nor displeasure nor joy nor pain."

Ultimately both of Danny's houses burn down, but too

late to redeem him. At a drunken party he charges out to "find the Enemy who is worthy of Danny" and finds only death. After his death the little band that he had assembled breaks up, "and no two walked together."

Steinbeck himself stresses in his preface the similarity of the cycle of *paisano* tales to the Arthurian legends; but the struggle in *Tortilla Flat* is not so much between the dedication to mystical virtue that the Round Table represented and the greed and lusts of the flesh that destroyed it as between natural impetuosity and the restraints of civilization. Steinbeck's point is that once one succumbs to the lure of property, he cannot hope to return to a state of primitive innocence. His equation of his characters to Arthurian knights, however, indicates what he considers the twentieth-century equivalents of the medieval situation.

The reader is distracted from the somber message of the novel, however, by the author's mock-heroic style and the characters' hilarious lack of inhibitions. Whatever the author may have intended, *Tortilla Flat* is valued today as a colorful genre piece rather than a moral fable. In Steinbeck's next two works, however, the gaiety vanishes; the social criticism becomes unmistakable. *In Dubious Battle* and *Of Mice and Men* are uncompromisingly brutal records of the harm done by those willing to suppress human feelings and aspirations violently in order to impose their own selfish vision upon the world.

Respectability takes on a broader meaning in these novels—which in retrospect mark the high point of Steinbeck's power as a fabulist—than in his earlier broadsides against bourgeois self-satisfaction. Steinbeck illustrates through these two powerful short novels that the Communist agitator and proto-Fascist hood have more in common with their implacable enemies among the respectable, complacent middle class than any would care to admit.

A long battle irrelevant to the novel's merits has raged around *In Dubious Battle* because of the failure of the Communist agitators in the novel to conform to the party line of the period. Steinbeck has patiently explained that he was interested in communism in action, not in theory; and what transpires in the field is rarely what is dreamed up in headquarters. Far from sympathizing with the agitators' effort to replace the present political system with another, he was trying to point out—through the speeches of Doc Burton, the most sympathetically presented character in the novel—that all systems contain the germ of their own destruction simply by dint of being systems. When one of the agitators, who has earlier told a young disciple, "We can't waste time liking people," later accuses Burton of not believing in "the cause," the challenged man replies:

> "That's like not believing in the moon. There've been communes before, and there will be again. But you people have an idea that if you can *establish* the thing, the job'll be done. Nothing stops, Mac. If you were able to put an idea into effect tomorrow, it would start changing right away."

"Nothing stops, Mac," with these words Doc Burton enunciates the conviction that underlies Steinbeck's writing. The novelist writes about the processes of life because he sees life as process. He objects to respectability, because it attempts to arrest this process, to freeze things into some sort of unnaturally maintained status quo. Doc Burton represents the scientific man of good will who believes in allowing the processes of life to operate and in moving along with them, observing and possibly channeling them, but never aborting them.

At the time he wrote *In Dubious Battle*, however, Steinbeck despaired of the fate of men of good will. Doc Burton is called out—perhaps as part of a deliberate plot—to attend a patient and simply disappears, as William Golding observes Lear's fool did. The one young agitator who might have been won to Burton's way of thinking has his face blown off by a shotgun blast and then suffers the ultimate indignity of having his faceless corpse exploited by his fellow agitators to whip up the irrational emotions of a mob.

Mob emotions play a prominent role also in the harrowing conclusion of *Of Mice and Men*, Steinbeck's first attempt to write a novel that could be staged without alteration. At first glance, this tense drama of the destruction of the dream of two itinerant ranch hands seems peopled by too disreputable a cast of characters to constitute even an implicit attack on respectability; but the vicious villain of the piece—a kind of rural juvenile delinquent who might ride today with "Hell's Angels"—shows, through the rigidity of his depraved code, how flexible are the applications of the term "respectability" (as John Gay had long ago in *The Beggar's Opera*).

The first time that we hear of Curley, the son of the owner of the ranch to which George and Lennie, the traveling hands, have fled from some catastrophe, we learn that he has his own distorted concept of respectability, since though he is constantly picking fights, he keeps his left glove full of Vaseline so that the hand will be soft for his wife. This common little girl, we learn also, has married him because of her own aspirations to respectability. "I wasn't gonna stay no place where I couldn't get nowhere or make something of myself," she tells the uncomprehending Lennie only minutes before her accidental but predictable death at his hands reveals, once "the discontent and ache for attention were all gone," a "sweet and young" face.

The jealousy and vanity of Curley and his wife destroy not just her, but the innocent dreams of others. They are not just bumpkins stirring up forces that they cannot control, they are symbolic of all those willing to destroy the world to gratify their own famished egos. It is hard to believe that *Of Mice and Men*—with its titular allusion to one of the great masterpieces of moralizing verse—simply appeared coincidentally at the time when Hitler was launching the series of defiant aggressions that turned the world into a holocaust. A remote California ranch becomes in Steinbeck's hands a microcosm for a world troubled by delusions of grandeur and paranoid suspicions.

During the same years in which he published *In Dubious Battle* and *Of Mice and Men*, Steinbeck also completed the work that is probably his most perfect allegory, the cycle of four stories called collectively *The Red Pony*. In these tales the realistic narrative and underlying fable are so perfectly fused that each word makes a precise and essential contribution to the author's double purpose—to depict through a series of nostalgic evocations of the environment the author himself knew as a child what I have called in *John Steinbeck* "a young man's emergence into compassionate adulthood by his painful learning through four personal experiences of the fallibility of man, the wearing out of man, the unreliability of nature, and the exhaustion of nature."

Through the depiction of the relationships between three

generations in these stories, Steinbeck also summarizes his attack on respectability and at the same time offers a glimpse of brighter hope for the future than he does in his longer works.

Jody Tiflin's grandfather is a man who has been devoted to the "processes of life," especially that one he calls "westering." Although he has been, as the title of the fourth story describes him, a "leader of the people," he has not sought this role to gratify his own vanity, but to serve others. "Every man wanted something for himself," the old man explains to Jody, "but the big beast that was all of them wanted only westering. I was the leader, but if I hadn't been there, someone else would have been the head." The important thing he recalls is that he carried the process forward as far as he could, " 'We carried life out here and set it down the way those ants carry eggs. . . . Then we came down to the sea, and it was done. . . . There's a line of old men along the shore hating the ocean because it's stopped them.' "

Jody's father, on the other hand, is a settled, respectable rancher, the kind of man who "insisted on giving permission for anything that was done on the ranch, whether it was important or not." He feels that when something is finished, "Nobody wants to hear about it over and over." He is a sedentary man, content to cultivate his fields. When Jody says it would be "good to go" to explore the wild mountains of their own country, which his father knows about only from reading, the father asks, "What for? There's nothing there."

Jody is thus exposed to the influence of both one who has—while the opportunity lasted—participated actively in advancing the processes of life and one who reads about the unknown but sees no reason to venture into it. The picture of Jody himself suggests that although Steinbeck felt that outlets for the spirit of "westering" had temporarily evaporated, the spirit itself had not disappeared. Although the disgruntled grandfather offers Jody no hope, the boy says, "Maybe I could lead the people some day."

Steinbeck achieves something like the fusion of realistic narrative and allegorical fable that distinguishes *The Red Pony* in the Joad chapters of *The Grapes of Wrath*. But even though this novel is generally conceded to be his greatest achievement, it has been subjected justly to one criticism that is not applicable to *In Dubious Battle, Of Mice and Men,* or *The Red Pony*: that the characters are too wise and articulate to be credible. Curiously critics have failed to perceive that this very criticism results from the novel's being basically allegorical rather than naturalistic. The characters are larger than life because Steinbeck is not simply photographing a particular migration but depicting through his portrayal of the Joads man in flight through the immemorial ages that his physical needs and his dreams have impelled him forward. It is particularly regrettable, therefore, that criticism of the novel has long been confused because, as Peter Lisca points out in *The Wide World of John Steinbeck*, "*The Grapes of Wrath* did not stand a chance of being accepted and evaluated as a piece of fiction. From the very beginning it was taken as substantial fact and its merits debated as a document rather than a novel."

I have already attempted to demonstrate in my book *John Steinbeck* that the story of the Joads is best read not as a document of a particular migration in the 1930's but as the story of the education of the principal characters "that results in a change from their jealously regarding themselves as an isolated and self-important family unit to their regarding themselves as part of a vast human family that . . . shares 'one big soul ever-body's a part of.'" I shall not retrace this evolution, however, for what is important about the novel from the point which I am now exploring in Steinbeck's work is the presentation therein of the force that frustrates the Joads' quest.

Steinbeck never argues that the Joads should simply have stayed home in Oklahoma and demanded relief. Rather he is anxious to get them on the road, westering, so that he can point out the obstacles to their achieving a new life. As in his earlier works, these are principally the forces of respectability. Although there are occasional jibes at the very wealthy, like the "newspaper fella near the coast, got a million acres," Steinbeck's darts are aimed principally at the respectable middle class, at "little pot-bellied men in light suits and panama hats," wearing "in their lapels the insignia of lodges and service clubs, places where they can go and, by a weight of numbers of worried little men, reassure themselves that business is noble and not the curious ritualized thievery they know it is."

Steinbeck directs his anger principally against the Californians, who "forgot the land, the smell, the feel of it, and remembered only that they owned it, remembered only what they gained and lost by it," who hated Okies because they had perhaps "heard from their grandfathers how easy it is to steal land from a soft man if you are fierce and hungry and armed." Steinbeck blames the conditions that he depicts on the "men of the towns and the soft suburban country," who "reassured themselves that they were good and the invaders bad . . . dirty, ignorant . . . degenerate."

Softness is the culprit that destroys the spirit of westering. Significantly, Steinbeck does not enable the Joads to stay in the Weedpatch government camp, the only place where they are treated with dignity, because they cannot find work there, and their own spirit might have deteriorated if they had been able to live off unearned bounty. Steinbeck is not interested in the possibility of achieving stationary arrangements that may preserve men without expanding their spirits. Even the Joads themselves, he has pointed out early in the book, have been largely responsible for their own troubles by becoming too attached to a settled way of life on the Oklahoma farm that they have allowed to deteriorate.

The only governmental arrangement that Steinbeck speaks of enthusiastically is by its very nature ephemeral. In chapter seventeen, in which he discusses the change in the social pattern of the life of the migrants—the kind of change he stresses that "in the whole universe" only man can make—he explains how in the camps the migrants set up "there grew up government ... with leaders, with elders. ... And a kind of insurance developed in these nights." He goes on to point out, however, that these "worlds built in the evening," disappear with morning and the people move on, not remaining in fixed groups but integrating "with any group they found."

He looks approvingly on only that form of government that arises out of the immediate needs of the people and remains in a continual state of evolutionary flux, an arrangement that would allow no opportunity for the development of fixed canons of respectability. Although far from urging anarchy (he insists upon the establishment of law and order even in overnight camps), he is opposed to any mode of government that can exist long enough to freeze into a system—to allow the establishment of castes, military cliques, presidential libraries. He rejects political organization as anything more than an expedient.

This rejection by many Americans from Thoreau (who said "I am as desirous of being a good neighbor as I am of being a bad subject") to Bob Dylan, whose disinterest in Viet Nam distressed his ideologically minded French admirers, has long been the despair of intellectual theorists who apparently cannot conceive of achieving an identity except as the product of a relationship to some external framework that can coagulate into a tradition. Steinbeck's novels deserve recognition as perhaps the outstanding fictional embodiments of a perennial American attitude.[2]

The high point of Steinbeck's one-man war on respectability is not, however, his monumental *The Grapes of Wrath*, but the less ambitious, seemingly whimsical work that grew some years later out of his disillusionment with World War II, *Cannery Row*. Few of his novels have been more grossly misinterpreted, because shocked readers have insisted upon taking his sympathetic treatment of bums, petty crooks, lechers, and prostitutes literally as a deliberate sentimentalization of the seedy side of life. Nowhere in the novel, however, does Steinbeck suggest that their way of life should be emulated. In one of the few places where we are allowed to peer behind the jolly façade of life along Monterey's waterfront, we hear Mack, ringleader of the bums, confess to the biologist who is beating him up for

[2] The tradition is not, of course, exclusively American, although it has flourished in this country. French artists are not always as preoccupied with ideology as French audiences. For example, one of Steinbeck's most audacious successors in the war against respectability is film director Jean-Luc Godard, whose *Alphaville* satirizes a society in which respectability becomes a norm strictly maintained by a controlling computer.

ruining a laboratory during a well-intentioned party that got out of hand, "It don't do no good to say I'm sorry. I been sorry all my life. This ain't no new thing. It's always like this . . . . I had a wife . . . . Same thing. Ever'thing I done turned sour . . . . Same thing ever' place 'til I just got to clowning. I don't do nothin' but clown no more. Try to make the boys laugh."

The raffish denizens of Cannery Row are fugitives from failure, but at least they know that they have failed. Steinbeck's point is not that they are enviably happy, but that they are better off than their respectable neighbors who pride themselves on the negative lives they lead: the prominent Mason who shoots an air gun at a flagpole skater, the observant gentleman who insists on the respectful burial of Josh Billings' insides, the "high-minded ladies" who demand "that dens of vice must close to protect young American manhood."

One of Steinbeck's sharpest blows at respectability is his portrait of a female legislator, whose kitchen Mack and the boys invade, "unconsciously glad she wasn't there," because "the kind of women who put paper on shelves and had little towels . . . instinctively distrusted and disliked Mack and the boys," who such women knew "were the worst threats to a home, for they offered ease and thought and companionship as opposed to neatness, order, and properness."

A more diverting, but perhaps even more devastating attack on the preoccupation with "neatness, order, and properness" is the portrayal of Mrs. Malloy, who once she is comfortably settled in a discarded boiler, renting out surrounding abandoned pipes, wants "things nice" and insists on buying curtains even though the boiler has no windows.

To stress the relationship between *The Grapes of Wrath* and *Cannery Row*, I have jumped over one of Steinbeck's most controversial works, *The Moon Is Down*, which is probably in some measure responsible for his winning the Nobel Prize, because of its popularity among Resistance fighters in Europe during World War II. Although the Europeans' sentimental enthusiasm for this tribute to their unvanquished spirit is understandable, American critics were justified in detecting in this second attempt of Steinbeck's to write a work that could be both read as a novel and acted as a play the beginning of a decline in his work.

The decline appears a result of Steinbeck's penchant for allegory at last overwhelming him. The books with California settings had been distinguished by a technique that permitted them to satisfy readers as either naturalistic accounts of rural life or as tragic allegories of man's universal experience. Even in *The Grapes of Wrath*, however, much of the material that I have quoted illustrative of the author's point of view comes not from the chapters telling the story of the Joads but from the frequently polemical interchapters that Steinbeck added to drive home directly the points that the fable of the Joads symbolized.

For some reason, when he came to write *The Moon Is Down*, Steinbeck insisted upon stressing its allegorical qualities by refusing to identify his characters specifically with the German invaders or the resistant citizens of a Norwegian village. This effort to stress the universality of the situation was, however, self-defeating, for as critics, notably James Thurber, pointed out, the characters became simply noble or villainous puppets. Some have attributed the novel's weakness to Steinbeck's lack of familiarity with the country and situation that he was writing about; but the evolution of his work since 1942 makes it appear more likely that he was simply succumbing to the occupational disease of fabulists frustrated because their messages have been ignored: he was beginning to strain too hard to make his points.

In *Cannery Row* he relaxed, recaptured, and, in fact, climaxed his old manner; but he has apparently never been willing to recognize that he is most effective as a heavily ironic humorist. Like many of the great satirists, he has sought honor as a tragedian, forgetting how much tragedy is rant. After *Cannery Row* the old Steinbeck, who brilliantly fused reality with allegory, was to reappear only once more in the droll, biting fable, "How Mr. Hogan Robbed a Bank." In his other works since the end of World War II, the urge to put his message across has submerged his ability to convey a message through stories about recognizably human characters moving against the powerfully evoked background of scenes that the author himself knew as a youth.

The trouble became manifest with the publication of *The Wayward Bus* (1946), a novel for which Steinbeck expressed high hopes. The progress of a busload of stereotyped postwar Americans from Rebel Corners to San Juan de la Cruz in the hands of a driver whose initials are J. C. so creaked with symbolism that few readers even bothered to figure out what might be the point of a story that was climaxed with copulation not for the fun of it, or even the sin of it, but to boost the participants' morales.

The novels that followed suggested that Steinbeck also

was no longer as clear as he had been about the identity of the forces that he was attacking. Asked by reporters during the interview following the announcement of the Nobel Prize about his penchant for writing about underdogs, he replied, "Thirty years ago you could tell an underdog. Today it is rather harder to recognize one."

His difficulties are especially apparent if one looks closely at *The Pearl*, that godsend to high-school program planners seeking desperately a recent novel clean enough for classroom use and simple enough for the less-gifted students to comprehend. The novel's simplicity is deceptive, for it is not really clear when a pearl diver named Paco throws away a great gem that he has found whether the gesture symbolizes his rejection of materialism or his loss of self-confidence as a result of the death of his child at the hands of his greedy enemies. It is difficult to tell whether he is following in the footsteps of Mack and the boys or of Sir Henry Morgan.

In either event, Steinbeck appears to be advocating the abandonment of the difficult road to self-improvement that he showed the Joads following in *The Grapes of Wrath* and suggesting instead that the underdog accept his condition with resignation. "Fear the time when the bombs stop falling while the bombers live—for every bomb is proof that the spirit has not died," Steinbeck wrote in *The Grapes of Wrath*. At the end of *The Pearl*, the spirit is dead. No wonder genteel schoolmarms approve it.

"Dead on arrival" is, unfortunately, the best term to describe the vast inert mass titled *East of Eden* upon which Steinbeck expended great effort. Some readers received the novel enthusiastically because of the effectiveness of the historical passages describing the growth of a farming family in the California settings that Steinbeck has always handled well. The tragic history of a pioneering effort to ship fresh lettuce to the East Coast remains to haunt the reader after the interminable philosophizing of a Chinese sage and the preposterous allegory of old man Adam and his rival twin sons have become confused memories. The trouble with this ambitious work is that narrative and allegory never fuse; long passages of history and philosophizing alternate (as in Aldous Huxley's *After Many a Summer Dies the Swan*), but instead of complementing each other, they simply get in each other's way.

The low point of Steinbeck's career has surely, however, been his third effort to write a novel that could be performed as a play, *Burning Bright*, a work that is purely allegorical in that it has no literally recognizable setting and no credibly human characters. Instead the same group of puppets turn up mysteriously traveling with a circus, running a farm, and operating a ship. Steinbeck apparently hoped by refusing to confine the action to any one setting to stress the message about universal brotherhood that he wanted to convey through the work, but he succeeded only in confusing much of the audience into thinking that circus performers spend the off season on farms and alienating those who especially valued the powerful evocations of landscape and local customs that had given life and meaning to his earlier fables.

What had happened? A number of theories have been offered to account for the surprisingly rapid deterioration of Steinbeck's artistry following World War II. My own is that the death of his most respected critic, Ed Ricketts, and Steinbeck's removal from his native California to New York had put him out of touch with the counsel and materials that accounted for his greatest successes.

A possibility worth pondering, however, is his admitted difficulty in recognizing underdogs in the postwar world. It was no longer easy to draw neat lines distinguishing the exploiters from the exploited. Steinbeck admitted to a *Newsweek* reporter at the time of the publication of *The Winter of Our Discontent* that many of the surviving Okies in California were probably now guilty of the very practices that had victimized them. His own new way of life in a New York town house and Long Island summer house could not have failed to force him, furthermore, into a kind of respectability himself. His pathetic or tongue-in-cheek account in *Travels with Charley* of his efforts to get back in touch with the common people by riding around the country in a freakish rig show the inevitable effect that financial success and family life had in incorporating him into the very social group that he had spent his most artistically productive years attacking.

His most recently published novel, *The Winter of Our Discontent* (1961), seems to me a result of his inability to keep his bearings in the postwar world in an environment that he knew only as a celebrity.

Earlier I have commented that "How Mr. Hogan Robbed a Bank" promised in 1956 a return to the old fusion of realistic humor and biting criticism in a compact fable. Steinbeck seemed to be learning how to handle effectively material drawn from his new urban environment, but—as I have commented in *Modern Fiction Studies* (Spring, 1965) —when he converted the story into a novel, "the light-hearted, tongue-in-cheek fun disappeared and so did the charm of the work."

The greatest change occurred, however, in the theme of the work. The short story had, like *Cannery Row*, satirized "the complacent respectability that allows itself to be victimized when it fails to recognize the individuality and ingenuity of the anonymous 'personnel' who it is fancied have become but faceless cogs in a mindless machine." Steinbeck chose to make the novel a study of the individual's difficulty in maintaining his integrity in an avaricious world. His finding is that such an effort cannot be successful, because the world is hopelessly corrupt. Ethan Allen Hawley, driven by personal despair at his inability to remain incorruptible to the brink of suicide, is held back only by the realization that he must continue to endure in order to pave the way for the possible hope that another generation might offer.

Steinbeck had thus returned to the very kind of self-realization novel that he had attempted with little success thirty years earlier. However, whereas Joseph Wayne in *To a God Unknown* elected—to borrow some phrases from Stekel by way of J. D. Salinger—"to die nobly" for a cause, Ethan Allen Hawley elects "to live humbly." A novelist might, of course, successfully change his literary tactics, though few have. *The Winter of Our Discontent* might, in fact, appear a more creditable effort than it does were there not the "Mr. Hogan" story to offer melancholy evidence that Steinbeck should have stuck to what he had been able to do well instead of shifting late in his career to a kind of approach that he has never handled successfully.

Why did he make the shift? Perhaps he thought frivolous satire and fantasy firmly rooted in a recognizable setting were not "respectable" enough for an elder statesman's long narrative inquiry into American morale. Certainly he overrated the dramatic potential of his subject matter. He failed to perceive that his grubby Long Islanders were not victims of forces that they were not sophisticated enough to control—like the characters in *Of Mice and Men, In Dubious Battle*, and even *The Grapes of Wrath*—but a crew of parasites like those he had successfully treated mock-heroically in *Tortilla Flat* and *Cannery Row*. He had seemingly lost the ability to regard his characters objectively enough to hit upon the proper tone for their presentation. The man who had once traveled with the migrant workers had become too secure and comfortable to mingle with the underdogs of the postwar world; one of the most unsatisfactory chapters in *Travels with Charley* describes Steinbeck's avoidance of the real storm center during a racial uprising in New Orleans. To put the matter bluntly, Steinbeck's social fables have lost their impact since World War II because he no longer knows at firsthand what he is talking about. Like Morgan in *Cup of Gold*, he has split. His greatness rested in his ability to transform the underdogs that he had known from personal experience into universal symbols, not in his penchant for pontificating about the "American character" as he does in his most recent picture book for the Christmas trade.

Did the Nobel Committee recognize the true basis of his distinction? To a limited extent. Like others, they praised him for his defense of the underdog. "His sympathies," the announcement of the award states, "always go out to the oppressed, the misfits, and the distressed; he likes to contrast the simple joy of life with brutal and cynical craving for money." "The Academy's reason for awarding the prize to John Steinbeck," it concludes, "reads as follows: 'For his at one and the same time realistic and imaginative writings, distinguished as they are by a sympathetic humor and social perception.'"

While this statement does recognize, as many critics have not, the mixture of realistic and allegorical qualities in Steinbeck's fiction, it does not suggest an adequate perception that his long sympathy for the oppressed and distressed was not so much a part of a politically oriented division of society into exploited and exploiter (as the phrases "simple joy of life" and "brutal and cynical craving for money" imply) as it was his feeling that some people were denied— by the very efforts of those who attempted to freeze society, on the basis of one political philosophy or another, into such categories—the uniquely human right to participate in life as a process and to evolve as their distinctive individual natures permitted.

In his speech accepting the Nobel Prize, Steinbeck did, however, point out the attitude that characterizes his best work when he said that the writer "is charged with exposing our many grievous faults and failures, with dredging up to the light our dark and dangerous dreams, for the purpose of improvement." He went on to express his continuing faith in the necessity of man's participating fully and freely in the evolutionary process of life. "I hold that a writer who does not passionately believe in the perfectibility of man," he said, "has no dedication nor any membership in literature." "Having taken God-like power," he concluded, after referring to the terrors unleashed by the atomic bomb, "we must seek in ourselves the responsibility and wisdom we once prayed some deity might have. Man himself has become our greatest hazard and our only hope."

So man indeed appeared in the darkly pessimistic *In Dubious Battle*, in the warmly optimistic *The Red Pony*, and in the ambiguous *The Grapes of Wrath*. If Steinbeck has not since risen to the heights that he did in these works born of the Depression, his Nobel acceptance speech indicates that he is still aware of the artistic achievement necessary to reach such heights. It is, of course, much easier for a writer, or anyone else, to explain what he would like to do than it is for him to do it.

Steinbeck was proposed for the Nobel Prize as early as 1945. He should have won it then, while *The Grapes of Wrath* was still vivid in the memory of his countrymen, *The Moon Is Down* still precious to the hearts of Europeans just freed from the Nazi scourge, and *Cannery Row* still fresh evidence of his ability at his most skillful to fuse realistic report with trenchant fable. But that he did not receive the award at the time it would have been most appropriate does not mean that he has somehow ceased to deserve it. The delay, like many, was regrettable; but, as Alba della Fazia puts it, the recipient was "qualified." May we continue to produce men who have done as much to merit such an award, regardless of when, if ever, they receive it.

BIBLIOGRAPHICAL NOTES

Nothing like an exhaustive listing of writings by and about these seven distinguished Americans is intended. Their abundant works and the abundance of works about most of them are adequately chronicled elsewhere. This is a highly selective account of the best of these writings that may serve as an immediate guide to those who we hope may be stimulated by these essays to explore further the literary careers of our Nobel laureates.

Those wishing to make comprehensive studies of the careers of these writers should begin with the bibliographical supplement to *The Literary History of the United States*, edited by Robert E. Spiller and others (New York; third edition, revised, 1963), which contains separate bibliographies of works by and about all these authors except Pearl Buck through 1958. Useful selective bibliographies may also be found in the full-length studies of each of these authors contained in the "Twayne United States Authors Series," published in New York, beginning in 1961. The individual volumes in this series will be mentioned in the

224

following accounts. Most of the writers discussed in this book are also the subjects of individual bibliographical essays in *Fifteen Modern American Authors*, edited by Jackson R. Bryer, to be published by the Duke University Press in spring, 1968.

Those interested in keeping up-to-date on scholarship concerning these authors are referred to the separate volumes of *American Literary Scholarship*, edited since 1964 by James Woodress and published by the Duke University Press. Faulkner and Hemingway are treated in separate essays; the other writers are discussed in surveys of scholarship concerning twentieth-century poetry, fiction, and drama.

SINCLAIR LEWIS

As Professor Griffin's essay suggests, Lewis' reputation rests mainly on the novels that he produced during the 1920's: *Main Street* (New York, 1920), *Babbitt* (New York, 1922), *Arrowsmith* (New York, 1925), *Elmer Gantry* (New York, 1927), *The Man Who Knew Coolidge* (New York, 1928), *Dodsworth* (New York, 1929). Some later novels remain of topical interest, especially *Work of Art* (New York, 1934), the anti-Fascist cautionary tale *It Can't Happen Here* (New York, 1935), *Kingsblood Royal* (New York, 1947), and *The God-Seeker* (New York, 1949).

Most of Lewis' essays are collected in *The Man from Main Street: A Sinclair Lewis Reader*, edited by Harry E. Maule and Melville H. Cane (New York, 1953). A selection from his letters appears under the title *From Main Street to Stockholm: Letters of Sinclair Lewis, 1919–1930*, edited by Harrison Smith (New York, 1952).

Lewis was rarely mentioned more than half-heartedly by

literary critics under the publication of Mark Schorer's monumental, commissioned biography, *Sinclair Lewis* (New York, 1961), a work that is in every way exemplary: handsomely written, exhaustive, often sympathetic but never indulgent. Schorer has also edited *Sinclair Lewis: A Collection of Critical Essays* (Englewood Cliffs, N.J., 1962) for the "Twentieth-Century Views" series, and he has provided a pamphlet, *Sinclair Lewis* (Minneapolis, 1963) for a series on American writers.

Most of the reliable criticism of Lewis is listed in the bibliography of Sheldon Norman Grebstein's *Sinclair Lewis* (New York, 1962), a part of the "Twayne United States Authors Series." D. J. Dooley has recently published *The Art of Sinclair Lewis* (Lincoln, Nebr., 1967). Carl Van Doren's *Sinclair Lewis: A Biographical Sketch* (Garden City, 1933) is an early, sympathetic work that remains useful.

On the subject of Lewis and the Nobel Prize, Professor Griffin recommends Erik Karlfeldt's "Why Sinclair Lewis Got the Nobel Prize," *Saturday Review of Literature*, VII (Jan. 10, 1931), 524–25; Sheldon N. Grebstein's "Sinclair Lewis and the Nobel Prize," *Western Humanities Review*, XIII (Spring, 1959), 163–71; and Carl F. Anderson's *The Swedish Acceptance of American Literature* (Philadelphia, 1957).

R. W. B. Lewis' *The American Adam* (Chicago, 1955) is most helpful in understanding Lewis' American background; his parallels with Dickens are suggested by George Orwell's writings about the British novelist.

EUGENE O'NEILL

O'Neill's reputation rests, like Sinclair Lewis', in a large measure on the works created before he won the Nobel Prize, but some posthumously produced plays are of great importance.

The principal plays on which O'Neill's reputation was based when he was awarded the Nobel Prize in 1936 are (dates given are those of the first performance): *Beyond the Horizon* (New York; Feb. 2, 1920), *The Emperor Jones* (New York; Nov. 1, 1920); *Anna Christie* (New York; Nov. 2, 1921); *The Hairy Ape* (New York; March 9, 1922), *Desire Under the Elms* (New York; Nov. 11, 1924); *The Great God Brown* (New York; Jan. 23, 1926); *Marco Millions* (New York; Jan. 9, 1928); *Strange Interlude* (New York; Jan. 30, 1928); *Lazarus Laughed* (Pasadena, Calif.; April 9, 1928); *Mourning Becomes Electra* (New York; Oct. 26, 1931), *Ah, Wilderness!* (New York; Oct. 2, 1933).

The last important work to be produced during O'Neill's life was *The Iceman Cometh* (New York; Oct. 9, 1946). Since his death several plays that have considerably added to his reputation have been performed: *Long Day's Journey into Night* (Stockholm; Feb. 10, 1956), *A Touch of the Poet* (Stockholm; March 27, 1957), *Hughie* (Stockholm; Sept. 18, 1958), and *More Stately Mansions* (Stockholm; Nov. 9, 1962).

The most comprehensive study of the playwright's career is *O'Neill* by Arthur and Barbara Gelb (New York, 1962). A listing of reviews of O'Neill's plays is provided by Jordan Y. Miller's *Eugene O'Neill and the American Critic* (Hamden, Conn., 1962), and the most useful reviews are reprinted in *Playwright's Progress: O'Neill and the Critics* (Chicago, 1965), edited by Professor Miller.

Two insightful recent critical studies of the playwright are Frederic I. Carpenter's contribution to the "Twayne

United States Authors Series." *Eugene O'Neill* (New York, 1964), and John Raleigh's contribution to the Southern Illinois University "Crosscurrents" series, *The Plays of Eugene O'Neill* (Carbondale and Edwardsville, 1965).

The development of O'Neill's reputation may be traced through the critical reactions found in Joseph T. Shipley's *The Art of Eugene O'Neill* (Seattle, 1928), Virgil Geddes' *The Melodramadness of Eugene O'Neill* (Brookfield, Conn., 1934), Sophus K. Winther's *Eugene O'Neill: A Critical Study* (New York, 1934), Richard D. Skinner's *Eugene O'Neill: A Poet's Quest* (New York, 1935); Barrett H. Clark's *Eugene O'Neill: The Man and His Plays* (New York, 1947), Edwin Engel's *The Haunted Heroes of Eugene O'Neill* (Cambridge, Mass., 1953); Doris V. Falk's *Eugene O'Neill and the Tragic Tension* (New Brunswick, N.J., 1958); Doris Alexander's *The Tempering of Eugene O'Neill* (New York, 1962), and Oscar Cargill, N. Bryllion Fagin, and William J. Fisher's *O'Neill and His Plays* (New York, 1962).

A useful background study is Helen Deutsch and Stella Hanau's history of *The Provincetown* (New York, 1931), the experimental theater where many of O'Neill's early plays were first performed. A collection of criticism appears in *O'Neill* (Englewood Cliffs, N.J., 1964), edited by John Gassner for the "Twentieth-Century Views" series.

PEARL BUCK

Mrs. Buck is a most prolific writer. She has produced at least one book nearly every year since 1930; in some years she has published three or four books. The only comprehensive listing of her books is to be found in the chronology at the beginning of Paul A. Doyle's *Pearl S. Buck*, a part of the "Twayne United States Authors Series" and at present the only book-length critical study of Mrs. Buck's life and works, although there is an earlier biography, *The Exile's Daughter* (New York, 1944), by Cornelia Spencer, a pseudonym for Mrs. Buck's sister, Grace S. Yaukey. This book contains no literary criticism, but a wealth of biographical details.

Mrs. Buck's reputation continues to rest on the series of novels that grew out of her observations of Chinese life: *The Good Earth* (New York, 1931), *Sons* (New York, 1932), *The Mother* (New York, 1934), *A House Divided* (New York, 1935), *The Patriot* (New York, 1939), *Dragon Seed* (New York, 1942), *Pavilion of Women* (New York, 1946), *Imperial Woman* (New York, 1956).

In recent years she has become particularly interested in the problems of retarded children, and she has written a great number of books about Chinese and American life for children. Her novels and nonfiction books about American life have never won the favor, however, that her novels and other books about China have. Since the end of World War II literary critics have accorded her work little recognition. Vito Brenni has contributed "Pearl Buck: A Selected Bibliography," however, to *Bulletin of Bibliography*, XXII (May–Aug., 1957) 65–69.

THOMAS STEARNS ELIOT

As Edmund Wilson observed somewhat deprecatingly, T. S. Eliot, despite his enormous reputation, has produced a relatively small body of work. His *Complete Poems and Plays, 1909–1950* (New York, 1952), which contains all of his creative writings through *The Cocktail Party*, is only 387 pages long. Besides this book, which contains "The

Love Song of J. Alfred Prufrock," *The Waste Land, Ash-Wednesday*, and *Four Quartets*, along with *Old Possum's Book of Practical Cats* and other major and minor works, his only creative works are the two late plays—*The Confidential Clerk* (New York, 1954) and *The Elder Statesman* (New York, 1958)—and a trivial gift-book, *The Cultivation of Christmas Trees* (New York, 1954).

Eliot's essays bulk much larger, and the *Selected Essays* (New York, 1952) contains only a small part of them. The most important of the many books of criticism that he has published are: *The Sacred Wood: Essays on Poetry and Criticism* (New York, 1920), which embodies the ideas that have probably most strongly influenced subsequent criticism; *For Lancelot Andrewes: Essays on Style and Order* (New York, 1928); *After Strange Gods* (New York, 1934); *The Idea of a Christian Society* (New York, 1939); *Notes Toward the Definition of Culture* (New York, 1948); and *On Poetry and Poets* (New York, 1957). A detailed listing of Eliot's writing can be found in Donald C. Gallup's *T. S. Eliot: A Bibliography, Including Contributions to Periodicals and Foreign Translations* (New York, 1953).

As Edmund Wilson also remarks, a formidable amount of criticism has been written about Eliot's small body of work. It is impossible even to suggest all the studies of substantial merit, but Professor Baker has designated the dozen that follow as those that he has found most useful and rewarding: F. O. Matthiessen, *The Achievement of T. S. Eliot* (Boston, 1935), the keystone of Eliot studies by the distinguished author of *American Renaissance*; Elizabeth Drew, *T. S. Eliot: The Design of His Poetry* (New York, 1949) and Helen L. Gardner, *The Art of T. S. Eliot* (London, 1949), highly influential studies by two of the greatest women students of modern poetry; Grover C. Smith, *T. S. Eliot's Poetry and Plays: A Study in Sources and Meanings* (Chicago, 1956), the standard account of the many sources in many cultures that Eliot drew upon in his work; Hugh Kenner, *The Invisible Poet: T. S. Eliot* (New York, 1959), a stimulating study by one of our most individualistic and outspoken critics; Staffan Bergsten, *Time and Eternity: A Study in the Structure and Symbolism of T. S. Eliot's "Four Quartets,"* a distinguished foreign contribution to the study of one of Eliot's greatest poetic achievements; David E. Jones, *The Plays of T. S. Eliot* (Toronto, 1960) and Carol H. Smith, *T. S. Eliot's Dramatic Theory and Practice* (Princeton, 1963), two studies of the form to which Eliot increasingly turned in his later life; Philip R. Headings, *T. S. Eliot* (New York, 1964), a part of the "Twayne United States Authors Series"; Georges Cattani, *T. S. Eliot*, translated from the French by Claire Pace and Jean Stewart (London, 1966), and Fei-Pai Lu, *T. S. Eliot: The Dialectical Structure of His Theory of Poetry* (Chicago, 1966), two further studies of the great Anglo-American writer by foreign scholars; and Leonard Unger, *T. S. Eliot: Moments and Patterns* (Minneapolis, 1966).

Professor Unger has also edited *T. S. Eliot: A Selected Critique* (New York, 1948), which reprints the works of a number of scholars. Many beginning readers of Eliot have found useful the poem-by-poem explications of his work in George Williamson's *A Reader's Guide to T. S. Eliot* (New York, 1949).

WILLIAM FAULKNER

Faulkner has possibly been even more talked about than Eliot. His works have been listed many times, and several indices to the characters in his works exist. The most analytical guide to his works remains James B. Meriwether's *The Literary Career of William Faulkner: A Bibliographical Study* (Princeton, 1961), an expanded version of an article in the Spring, 1957, issue of the *Princeton University Library Chronicle*.

Faulkner published twenty-eight books, but his reputation rests mainly on the fourteen books that, together with some short stories and supplementary works, make up the Yoknapatawpha saga, about a mythical Mississippi county that closely resembles Lafayette County, where Faulkner spent much of his life. These novels are: *Sartoris* (New York, 1929), *The Sound and the Fury* (New York, 1929), *As I Lay Dying* (New York, 1930), *Sanctuary* (New York, 1931), *Light in August* (New York, 1932), *Absalom, Absalom!* (New York, 1936), *The Unvanquished* (New York, 1938), *The Hamlet* (New York, 1940), *Go Down, Moses and Other Stories* (New York, 1942), *Intruder in the Dust* (New York, 1948), *Requiem for a Nun* (New York, 1951), *The Town* (New York, 1957) and *The Mansion* (New York, 1959)—which with *The Hamlet* comprise the "Snopes Trilogy," and *The Reivers* (New York, 1962).

Faulkner's first publication was a book of poems, *The Marble Faun* (Boston, 1924); his first novel was *Soldiers' Pay* (New York, 1926). One of his most ambitious but least admired works is the novel *A Fable* (New York, 1954). His short stories are gathered from several books in *Collected Stories of William Faulkner* (New York, 1950). His miscellaneous writings have been collected in *Essays, Speeches and Public Letters of William Faulkner*, edited by James B. Meriwether (New York, 1965).

Joseph Blotner has been commissioned to prepare an

official biography of Faulkner. In the meantime, one can learn much about Faulkner's early life from *My Brother Bill* by John Faulkner (New York, 1963). Faulkner's comments on his work are preserved in several books, most notably *Faulkner at the University*, edited by Frederick L. Gwynn and Joseph L. Blotner (Charlottesville, Va., 1959). The recollections of his friends and neighbors are recorded in *William Faulkner of Oxford*, edited by James W. Webb and A. Wigfall Green (Baton Rouge, La., 1965). An especially valuable correspondence, revealing many of Faulkner's ideas about writing, is presented in Malcolm Cowley's *The Faulkner-Cowley File: Letters and Memories, 1944–1962* (New York, 1966).

This correspondence concerns the compilation of *The Portable Faulkner* (New York, 1946; revised edition, 1967), in which Cowley presents excerpts from Faulkner's work arranged by the historical era that they depict in order to show how the once neglected novelist had presented through his fiction a history of the tormented conscience of his region. The Yoknapatawpha cycle of stories, the heart of Faulkner's work, is also examined in great detail in Cleanth Brooks' *William Faulkner: The Yoknapatawpha Country* (New Haven, 1963), the first of a two-volume study that should serve as the base for future studies of Faulkner.

Many other books and articles about Faulkner have appeared. Useful collections of criticisms of the author are *William Faulkner: Two Decades of Criticism* (East Lansing, 1951) and *William Faulkner: Three Decades of Criticism* (East Lansing, 1960), both edited by Frederick J. Hoffman and Olga W. Vickery. Both editors have also written valuable separate monographs on Faulkner. Hoffman's book *William Faulkner* (New York, 1961; revised edition, 1966) was the inaugural volume in the "Twayne United States Authors Series" and contains valuable bibliographical comments. Mrs. Vickery's *The Novels of William Faulkner* (Baton Rouge, 1959; revised edition, 1965) is described by Hoffman as the "best critical study of Faulkner." There is also a collection of critical essays, *Faulkner* (Englewood Cliffs, N.J., 1966), edited by Robert Penn Warren for the "Twentieth Century Views" series.

More than a dozen other books about Faulkner have appeared in this country alone. Harry M. Campbell and Ruel E. Foster's *William Faulkner: A Critical Appraisal* (Norman, Okla., 1951) was the first to appear and is still valuable for its study of Faulkner's humor and cosmic pessimism. Campbell taught in Oxford, where Faulkner lived. Ward L. Miner's *The World of William Faulkner* (Durham, N.C., 1952) presents valuable information about the relationship of Faulkner's books to the region in which he lived. Faulkner's own publisher has sponsored two studies of his work: Irving Howe's *William Faulkner: A Critical Study* (New York, 1952; revised edition, 1962) and Michael Millgate's *The Achievement of William Faulkner* (New York, 1965), which contains the greatest amount of biographical information of any of the books available at present. Lawrance Thompson's *William Faulkner: An Introduction and Interpretation* (New York, 1963), part of an "American Writers and Critics Series," is one of the better introductions to the writer. Joseph Gold's *William Faulkner: A Study in Humanism from Metaphor to Discourse* (Norman, Okla., 1966) deals especially with Faulkner's work since World War II.

ERNEST HEMINGWAY

Hemingway has been only a little less studied than

Faulkner; and far more biographical studies and reminiscences of him have been written, many of dubious value prepared hurriedly to capitalize upon his sensational death in 1961.

Like almost all the writers discussed in this volume, Hemingway did his best work in the early years of his literary career. His reputation still rests principally on two novels about the "lost generation"—*The Sun Also Rises* (New York, 1926) and *A Farewell to Arms* (New York, 1929). The merit of his later works remains controversial. Few critics care for *To Have and Have Not* (New York, 1937). The big novel about the Spanish Civil War, *For Whom the Bell Tolls* (New York, 1940) has many admirers, but some detractors. Opinion is even more divided about *The Old Man and the Sea* (New York, 1952), which some consider a great work and others a thin tour de force; but almost no one respects Hemingway's novel about World War II, *Across the River and Into the Trees* (New York, 1950).

Still among Hemingway's most highly regarded works are his short stories, collected under the title *The Short Stories of Ernest Hemingway* (New York, 1942). Also of particular interest are three nonfictional memoirs: *Death in the Afternoon* (New York, 1932), rising out of the author's interest in bullfighting; *Green Hills of Africa* (New York, 1935), rising out of the author's interest in big-game hunting; and the posthumously published *A Moveable Feast* (New York, 1964), an account of early friendships in Paris.

Two books are central to the critical study of Hemingway: Carlos Baker's *Hemingway: The Writer as Artist* (Princeton, 1952; third edition, revised, 1963), an elaborate study by the scholar who has since been designated Hemingway's official biographer; and *Ernest Hemingway, A Reconsideration* (New York, 1952; revised edition, University Park, Pa., 1966), by Philip Young, an exciting, iconoclastic scholar who also prepared *Ernest Hemingway* (Minneapolis, 1959), for the University of Minnesota series of pamphlets on American writers.

Baker and Young have managed to keep themselves at the center of the rather turbulent critical debate over Hemingway. Baker has edited the enormously useful *Ernest Hemingway: Critiques of Four Major Novels* (New York, 1962), and Young has surveyed somewhat caustically recent Hemingway scholarship in "Our Hemingway Man," *Kenyon Review*, XXVI (Nov., 1964), 676–707, and told of the difficulties he had with the subject over the publication of his own book in "Hemingway and Me," *Kenyon Review*, XXVIII (Jan., 1966), 15–37.

Other critical works, however, also provide valuable insights. Charles A. Fenton's *The Apprenticeship of Ernest Hemingway* (New York, 1954) is one of the most thorough and sensitive biographical studies. Lillian Ross's *Portrait of Hemingway* (New York, 1961) derives from a "Profile" published in the *New Yorker* in 1950. John Killinger's *Hemingway and the Dead Gods: A Study in Existentialism* (Lexington, Ky., 1961) relates the novelist to the fashionable postwar intellectual movement. Earl Rovit, a scholar who is also a widely acclaimed novelist himself, prepared *Ernest Hemingway* (New York, 1963) for the "Twayne United States Authors Series." Joseph de Falco's *The Hero in Hemingway's Short Stories* (Pittsburgh, 1963) studies these popular works in the terms of the currently popular myth criticism. Nelson Algren's *Notes from a Sea Diary:*

Hemingway All the Way (New York, 1965) is perhaps the most baroque and refreshing of the many meditations over the novelist published since his death; but it has been largely eclipsed by the sensation accompanying the publication of A. E. Hotchner's *Papa Hemingway, a Personal Memoir* (New York, 1966), a book that Hemingway's family and friends found offensive but the public loved.

JOHN STEINBECK

Steinbeck was nominated for the Nobel Prize in 1945; many people think that he should have won it then, if at all. Certainly his work has greatly declined in quality since the end of World War II. His reputation rests—like Faulkner's—on the stories that he wrote in the 1930's and 1940's about the region in which he grew up. The beautiful, but strife-torn valleys of California are the setting for *The Pastures of Heaven* (New York, 1932); *To a God Unknown* (New York, 1933), *Tortilla Flat* (New York, 1935); *In Dubious Battle* (New York, 1936); *Of Mice and Men* (New York, 1937), published in both novel and play form; *The Long Valley* (New York, 1938), a collection of short stories that includes "The Red Pony" cycle, which many critics consider Steinbeck's finest work; *The Grapes of Wrath* (New York, 1939); and *Cannery Row* (New York, 1945). *The Wayward Bus* (New York, 1947) and *East of Eden* (New York, 1952) are among Steinbeck's most ambitious works about agricultural California, but they are not as well regarded as the earlier books. His latest novel, *The Winter of Our Discontent* (New York, 1961) deals, with no great success, with the morality of the area in which he now lives on Long Island.

Steinbeck has written a number of nonfiction works, the most important of which is "The Log" from *Sea of Cortez* (New York, 1941; "The Log" was reprinted separately in 1951), which describes Steinbeck's "non-teleological" philosophy. *Travels with Charley in Search of America* (New York, 1962) is an enormously popular, but superficial account of a tour to "rediscover" the country. Steinbeck's latest publication, *America and Americans* (New York, 1966) is an elaborate picture book, containing an essay expressing Steinbeck's disapproval with much of contemporary life.

Relatively few books have been written about Steinbeck. Harry T. Moore's *The Novels of John Steinbeck: A First Critical Study* (Chicago, 1939) is still valuable as a cool appraisal of the novelist at the height of his popularity. Peter Lisca's *The Wide World of John Steinbeck* (New Brunswick, N.J., 1958), prepared with assistance from Steinbeck's agents and editor, is the fullest account so far of the author's life and work. Warren French's *John Steinbeck* (New York, 1961) is one of the earliest volumes in the "Twayne United States Authors Series." Joseph Fontenrose's *John Steinbeck: An Introduction and Interpretation* (New York, 1963) is a valuable short study by a classical scholar who knows the California settings of Steinbeck's work well.

Locating works about Steinbeck has been vastly simplified by the recent publication of *John Steinbeck: A Concise Bibliography (1930–1965)*, compiled by Tetsumaro Hayashi (Metuchen, N.J., 1967). Much of the most valuable criticism has been collected in *Steinbeck and His Critics: A Record of Twenty-Five Years*, edited by E. W. Tedlock, Jr., and C. V. Wicker (Albuquerque, 1957). Background information about Steinbeck's major novel is collected in *A Companion to "The Grapes of Wrath,"* edited by Warren French (New York, 1963), which includes the newspaper stories that Steinbeck wrote about the migrant workers.

THE CONTRIBUTORS

JAMES V. BAKER, professor of English, University of Houston, was born in Reading, England, in 1903. He holds the M.A. in History from Oxford (1929) and the Ph.D. in English from the University of Michigan (1954). Besides poems, articles, and reviews in literary magazines, he has published *A Book of Songs and Meditations* (London, 1924) and *The Sacred River: Coleridge's Theory of Imagination* (1957). He won the major Hopwood award for poetry at the University of Michigan in 1947, and he has served since 1960 as poetry editor of the University of Houston *Forum*.

WARREN FRENCH is chairman of the Department of English in the University of Missouri at Kansas City. Born in Philadelphia in 1922, he was educated at the Universities of Pennsylvania and Texas. Besides articles and book reviews, he has published *John Steinbeck* (1961), *Frank Norris* (1962), *J. D. Salinger* (1963), *A Companion to "The Grapes of Wrath"* (1963), *The Social Novel at the End of an Era* (1966), *The Thirties: Fiction, Poetry, Drama* (1967), and

Season of Promise (1968). He has served on the editorial boards of *Twentieth Century Literature, College Composition and Communication,* and the *Midcontinent American Studies Journal.*

ROBERT J. GRIFFIN is assistant professor of English in Yale University. Born in Tallahassee, Florida, he was educated at George Washington University, and the Universities of Florida and California (Berkeley), from which he received his Ph.D degree. Although his dissertation concerns Oliver Goldsmith, he has published articles on Shakespeare, Sackville, Whitman, Henry James, Faulkner, and Steinbeck, as well as eighteenth-century writers in *College English, JEGP, Neuphilologische Mitteilungen, Studies in English Literature, Essays in Modern American Literature,* and other scholarly serials. He has edited a collection of critical essays on Sinclair Lewis' *Arrowsmith* for the new "Twentieth Century Interpretations" series.

FREDERICK J. HOFFMAN was at the time of his death, December 24, 1967, Distinguished Professor of English in the University of Wisconsin–Milwaukee. Born in Wisconsin in 1909, he was educated at Stanford, Minnesota, and Ohio State universities. He was one of the most prolific and penetrating writers on twentieth-century American and French literature. His major works include *Freudianism and the Literary Mind* (1945), *The Little Magazine: A History and a Bibliography* (1946), *The Modern Novel in America* (1951), *The Twenties* (1955), *William Faulkner* (1961), *Gertrude Stein* (1961), *Conrad Aiken* (1962), *Samuel Beckett* (1962), *The Mortal No: Death and the Modern Imagination* (1964), *The Art of Southern Fiction* (1967), *The Imagination's New Be-*

ginning: Theology and Modern Literature (1967). He also edited collections of criticism of William Faulkner and F. Scott Fitzgerald.

WALTER E. KIDD was born in eastern Oregon. He received his B.A. and M.A. degrees from the University of Oregon and the Ph.D. from the University of Denver. He is professor of English and Resident Writer at Stephen F. Austin State College, Nacogdoches, Texas. Under the pen name "Conrad Pendleton," he has written three books of poetry: *Slow Fire of Time* (1956), *Time Turns West* (1961), and *West: Manhattan to Oregon* (1966), plus *Adventures of Frelf* (1964), a novelette. Besides publishing many poems, stories, articles, and reviews in literary magazines, he has been guest editor of *Voices* and *South and West, An International Quarterly*, a principal editor of *Twentieth Century Literature*, and editor for five years of the *PHSTA Magazine*.

JORDAN Y. MILLER is professor and assistant head of the Department of English in Kansas State University, Manhattan. Born in Manhattan in 1919, he was educated at Yale and Columbia, from which he received his Ph.D degree. His principal publications are *American Dramatic Literature* (1961), *Eugene O'Neill and the American Critic* (1962), *Playwright's Progress; O'Neill and the Critics* (1965). He is at work on a book on Elmer Rice and a long study of World War II drama. He reviews for *Modern Drama*, and is active in local community theater work as actor and director. He was Fulbright lecturer in Bombay, India, in 1964–65.

KENNETT MORITZ, as staff marketing manager for TRW Systems Group in Redondo Beach, California, is responsible for communicating the essential features of TRW's advanced technology in spacecraft and systems engineering. He was born in Seattle and received his Ph.D degree from the University of Washington. His dissertation subject was *Dickens and Film*. He taught English literature for six years in the University of Southern California, and in 1961 received the Distinguished Teaching Award for teaching excellence. He conducted the semester-long "Ernest Hemingway in Our Time" television course on the CBS Odyssey series and published *A Study Guide* to Hemingway.

Dody Weston Thompson is a free-lance writer in Los Angeles, currently engaged in preparing a commissioned series of 16mm. films for classroom use. Born and reared in New Orleans, she attended Sophie Newcomb and Black Mountain colleges. Her interest in things Chinese grows out of her research in Oriental affairs during World War II for the West Coast Office of War Information. She took up photography under Edward Weston and helped found *Arperture*, a serious photographic magazine. Her work is represented in museum and private collections. She edited a portion of Weston's journals and wrote the introductory essay for his *My Camera on Point Lobos*.

INDEX